W9-BNG-774

HINDUISM
WORLD RELIGIONS

by Madhu Bazaz Wangu

Facts On File
New York • Oxford

HINDUISM
World Religions

Facts On File, Inc.
460 Park Avenue South
New York, NY 10016
USA

Facts On File Limited
Collins Street
Oxford OX4 1XJ
United Kingdom

Wangu, Madhu Bazaz
    Hinduism / by Madhu Bazaz Wangu.
        p.   cm. — (World religions)
    Includes bibliographical references (p. 126) and index.
    Summary: Presents the history, customs, and beliefs of Hinduism, describing the mysteries and myths that sustained its growth over the centuries.
        ISBN 0-8160-2447-2
        1. Hinduism — Juvenile literature.   [1. Hinduism.]   I. Title.   II. Series.
JUV   BL1203.W35   1991
    294.5 — dc20   90-25431

R009169 5034

British CIP data available on request from Facts On File.

Facts On File books are available at special discounts when purchased in bulk quantities for businesses, associations, institutions or sales promotions. Please contact the Special Sales Department of our New York office at 212/683-2244 (dial 800/322-8755 except in NY, AK, or HI).

Developed by Brown Publishing Network, Inc.
Design Production by Jennifer Angell/Brown Publishing Network, Inc.
Photo Research by Sue McDermott
Photo credits:
Cover: Painting, **Krishna Fluting**, The Kanoria Collection, ACSAA slide © AAAUM.
Title page: Morning prayers in the Ganges, John Henebry.
Table of Contents page: Shiva Nataraga, Delhi National Museum, Giradoun/Art Resource, NY.
Pages 6-7 John Henebry; 11 John Henebry; 12 Madhu Bazaz Wangu; 14-15 Robert & Linda Mitchell; 17 ACSAA slide © AAAUM; 19 John Henebry; 24-25 John Henebry; 27 Ken Laffal; 34 Ross-Coomaraswamy Collection, courtesy, Museum of Fine Arts, Boston; 39 John Henebry; 42-43 ACSAA slide © AAAUM; 44 By courtesy of the Board of Trustees of the Victoria & Albert Museum; 55 John Henebry; 58 ACSAA slide © AAAUM; 62 Madhu Bazaz Wangu; 68-69 AP/Wide World; 73 John Henebry; 79 AP/Wide World; 84-85 SEF/Art Resource, NY; 88 Clemens Kalischer; 93 John Henebry; 94 Reuters/Bettmann; 97 Clemens Kalischer; 100-101 Madhu Bazaz Wangu; 110 (left) John Henebry; 110 (right) Robert & Linda Mitchell; 112 Madhu Bazaz Wangu; 116-117 UPI/Bettmann; 121 UPI/Bettmann.

Printed in the United States of America
10 9 8 7 6 5 4 3 2 1
This book is printed on acid-free paper

TABLE OF CONTENTS

Preface

The 20th century is sometimes called a "secular age," meaning, in effect, that religion is not an especially important issue for most people. But there is much evidence to suggest that this is not true. In many societies, including the United States, religion and religious values shape the lives of millions of individuals and play a key role in politics and culture as well.

The World Religions series, of which this book is a part, is designed to appeal to both students and general readers. The books offer clear, accessible overviews of the major religious traditions and institutions of our time. Each volume in the series describes where a particular religion is practiced, its origins and history, its central beliefs and important rituals, and its contributions to world civilization. Carefully chosen photographs complement the text, and a glossary and bibliography are included to help readers gain a more complete understanding of the subject at hand.

Religious institutions and spirituality have always played a central role in world history. These books will help clarify what religion is all about and reveal both the similarities and differences in the great spiritual traditions practiced around the world today.

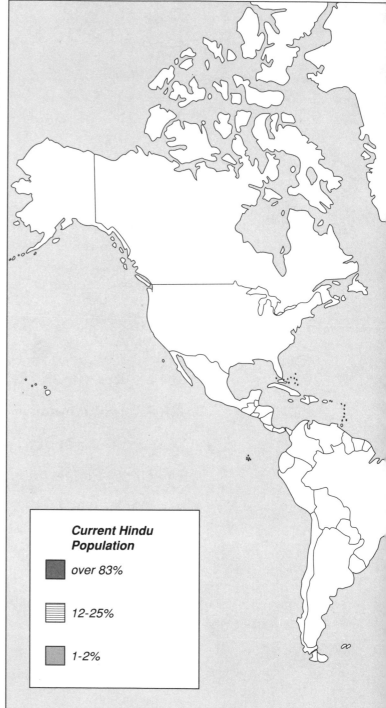

Current Hindu Population

over 83%

12-25%

1-2%

CHAPTER 1

Introduction: The Modern Hindu World

*H*induism is one of the oldest religions in existence. After Christianity and Islam, it ranks as the world's third largest religion. Today there are about 650 million Hindus worldwide.

The majority of Hindus live in India, where the religion was born. There are also significant Hindu minorities in Bangladesh and Pakistan, and smaller groups can be found in Sri Lanka, Indonesia, Fiji, Africa, Great Britain, Canada, and the United States. While Hindus in each of these societies have altered their religion to suit the needs of their cultures, all Hindus share a core of rich, poetic, and complex traditions.

Unlike Buddhism, Confucianism, Taoism, Christianity, Islam, or most of the other active world religions, Hinduism was not founded by one individual. Rather, it is the result of a coming together of many religious beliefs and philosophical schools. The different schools of thought and doctrine that flourished on Indian soil over the centuries were not originally labeled as Hindu. Nor was there a religion called Hinduism. The name *Hindu* came into use when the Persians, in their attempt to label all non-Muslim people living beyond the Sindhu river, mispronounced the word *Sindhu*.

In later centuries, Arabs, Turks, Afghans, and Mughals—all Muslims—used the term *Hindu* just for the sake of convenience. In their view of the world, there were the believers of Islam and "the rest." Hindus were, therefore, "the rest," and Hinduism was considered to be the religion of all non-Muslims. It is important to note that all of those who were grouped together as "the rest"were not Hindus. As mentioned, Hinduism was a particular religion that gradually developed among the non-Muslims.

Early Hinduism combined the religions of the Indus Valley in northwestern India with that of Aryan invaders from Persia. Later, Hinduism developed a more solid foundation through the writing and interpretation of the great Hindu scriptures. Throughout its many years, Hinduism has also developed as a result of the challenges of foreigners. India found itself conquered and ruled repeatedly by foreign invaders—Arabs, Turks, Afghans, Mughals, and the British. The unique cultures and religions of these invaders have had an effect on the ideas and principles of Hinduism. Yet, despite these many influences, and the changes that came to pass, India has remained essentially Hindu.

The Gods and the Scriptures

From its beginnings, Hinduism has been a polytheistic religion, meaning that its followers believe in many gods. Some people estimate the number of Hindu gods to be in the thousands. Others suggest that though innumerable minor gods exist, there is really only one true "god" at the heart of Hinduism—*Brahman*. Brahman is also called the One, the Ultimate Reality, and the World Soul. According to this interpretation, the many gods traditionally found in Hinduism really form part of Brahman.

The Hindus have come to know about their many gods by listening to and reading an enormous body of sacred literature. They have never followed the teachings contained in a single holy book, such as the Bible of Judaism and Christianity or the Koran of Islam. Although at the beginning of the twentieth century, western scholars working on ancient Hindu literature tried to isolate a "Hindu Bible" and believed that they were successful in identifying the *Bhagavad Gita* as the holy book, more recent scholars recognize that no single text is most important.Hinduism recognizes several sacred writings, all of which contribute to basic Hindu beliefs.

There are two main categories of Hindu scripture—*shruti*, "that which is heard," and *smriti*, "tradition" or "that which is to be remembered." The *Vedas* and the *Upanishads* fall into the category of shruti. These sacred writings are considered to be inspired by God and to have been revealed to humankind by ancient sages called *rishis*.

Each of the shruti texts provides an important part of the foundation of Hinduism. The four *Vedas* are the oldest of the texts and are the primary scriptures of Hinduism. It is difficult to assign exact dates to these writings, because many were compiled gradually, over centuries, through oral tradition. They were written down only long after they had come into existence. One of the four *Vedas* contains hymns, chants, and praises to the gods. Another *Veda* serves as a guidebook for rituals and priestly behavior. A third offers information on magic and charms that can be used as blessings or curses, and the fourth gives musical notes to be chanted while performing the rituals. Together, the four *Vedas* have had a deep and lasting influence on Hinduism. The *Brahmanas* were texts composed after the *Vedas*. These texts give the details of the routines to be followed during the fire sacrifices. *Aranyakas* "the forest books" composed after *Brahamanas* emphasize only the meaning of rituals.

The *Upanishads*, the latest of the shruti scriptures, were written around 700-500 B.C.E. One meaning for the word *Upanishad* is "sitting down near" a *guru* (spiritual master) who passes on his secret teachings. Almost all *Upanishads* are written in the form of dialogues between a student and a teacher. Indeed, many of the Upanishadic teachings were to become permanent elements of Hinduism. Most important of these are the concepts of *karma* (on's deeds will later have an affect in this life or in another life), *samsara* (reincarnation, or the cycles of a soul's birth and rebirth), and *moksha* (release from the cycles of samsara). In addition, the *Upanishads* questioned the nature of both *atman* (the soul of the individual) and *brahman* (the Universal Soul), and their relationship to one another. These questions have played an important role in the development and practice of Hinduism.

Because of their divine origin, shruti texts are considered to be more sacred than the other class of scriptures, smriti. Works that come after the *Vedas* and the *Upanishads* are all smriti. These include epics, *Puranas, Sutras, Shastras*, and devotional *Bhakti* songs.

India boasts of two great smriti epics. Both of them, the *Mahabharata* and the *Ramayana*, have had a significant influence on Hindu thought. These two epics have had many layers added to them over the centuries, and both have undergone numerous changes.

The *Mahabharata*, containing over ninety thousand stanzas, is probably the longest epic poem in history. According to Hindu tradition, the sage Vyasa dictated it to Ganesha, the elephant-god of good luck and wisdom and the patron of learning. It tells the story of two families engaged in war. It includes the *Bhagavad Gita*, an important sacred text in Hinduism which tells an important story about the god Krishna.

The other great epic, the *Ramayana* ("the goings of Rama"), tells the tale of Rama, the seventh incarnation of the god Vishnu. The Ramayana depicts the ideals of faithfulness to marriage vows, brotherly affection, and loyalty. The earliest parts of the text date from around 350 B.C.E., but the work as a whole was not compiled until much later. Both the *Mahabharata* and the *Ramayana* have influenced the philosophy of Hinduism for over two thousand years.

The *Puranas*—literally "something very old"—are also smriti writings. Written in Sanskrit, these form a collection of verses that tell the stories of Hinduism's best known gods and goddesses and the lives of ancient heroes. They include creation stories, portraits of the gods and famous sages, and accounts of time periods ruled by semi-gods called *manus*. They also speak of the end of the world and its rebirth, the history of humankind, and the legends of ancient dynasties. The *Puranas* are referred to as the *Vedas* of the common people, because they present traditional religious and historical material through tales that most Hindus can understand.

Another popular form of scripture is the *Bhakti* literature. These devotional songs were produced in both southern and northern regions of India, where teachers emphasized the love of those devoted to a personal god or goddess and the love returned by the god or goddess. The Bhakti movement developed a number of poet-sages who sang praises to Hindu gods and goddesses in the languages of the common people. By the sixth century C.E., these devotional hymns were being sung in many temples. Even today, many Hindus write and sing Bhakti hymns.

The Hindu scriptures, and the stories they contain, guide Hindus in their daily lives. They also help to preserve the religious dimensions of family and society. From these texts, and from their interpretations, Hindus have developed their system of worship and beliefs.

Hindu Worship and Beliefs

Three major sects comprise Hinduism, each based on a different idea of the divine, the universe, and the human condition. These sects are each represented by a high god—Shiva, Vishnu, or Shakti—and are referred to as Shaivism, Vaishnavism, and Shaktism, respectively. The different sects of Hinduism are loosely bound together by a single belief: they recognize that many different and individual paths may lead to the one ultimate goal of Hinduism, *moksha*, which is release from the attachment people have to this material world. Each sect lays out its own way of attaining moksha's reward—a blissful union with the universal spirit of Brahman.

Some important rituals, beliefs, and traditions keep the religion vital and hold all the sects of Hinduism together. These are *puja*, or daily worship; *dharma*, religious duties pertaining to family and society; *samskara*, rites of passage; *samsara*, belief in the reincarnation or reappearance of the soul in succeeding generations; and *moksha*, or final release from material existence.

Each day, Hindus worship the divine—either a high god or a family deity. To do this, they perform puja in a sacred corner in a worship room of the home. The puja ritual keeps Hindus aware of their gods and mindful of their duties as individuals.

The most exalted setting for performing puja is the temple. The temple is the house of god and a link between human existence and the divine. It is also the center of social, artistic,

■ *People crowd into a small Ganesha shrine. The statue of the god, placed on a high pedestal, overlooks his devotees. In the upper right-hand corner is a large metal bell that devotees ring as they enter the temple.*

■ *Devotees perform a special kind of ritual, called* **Puja**, *which involves all the senses. Lighted earthen lamps evoke the sense of sight; the sound of a bell evokes the sense of hearing; fragrant leaves and flowers evoke the sense of smell; ritual objects evoke the sense of touch; and finally, consumption of blessed food evokes the sense of taste.*

intellectual, and religious affairs. Most essentially, for a Hindu, the temple is a place of passage from this world to the next.

As early as the Vedic period, Hindu society was roughly divided into four divisions based on occupations. This basic part of Hindu life is known as the *caste system*. The Hindu caste system was supported by *dharma*, early religious laws of duty. Dharma insisted that particular castes had certain duties within the society. An individual, as a member of a caste, was responsible for upholding those duties. To neglect them was considered a sin that would upset the balance of life in the universe. Early Hindus believed, as do many modern Hindus, that if everyone were to performed his or her duty unquestioningly, a balance could be maintained in the world and humans could exist in peace.

More recently, the laws binding people to respect the caste system have loosened. As a result, modern dharma focuses more on duties to family than to society. Today, the family unit is considered especially sacred, and the fulfillment of obligations to the family is a religious duty.

Within every family and throughout society, individual life is divided into four stages—childhood, youth, middle age and old age. Hindus practice *samskara*, traditional rites of passage, to mark these important transitions from the moment of conception to the time of death. All rites of passage, including those of death and afterlife, are performed at home by the head of the household. According to tradition, each family member is responsible for maintaining sacred order in the family, in society, and ultimately in the universe, and the celebration of these rites of passage are part of that order. Religious observance of the basic rites (conception and birth, introduction to the guru for initiation, marriage, and cremation after death) are believed to be part of the path that leads Hindus toward their goal of moksha.

In their pursuit of moksha, Hindus share the ultimate goal of being spiritually united with the Ultimate Reality—*Brahman*. Thus, Hindus consider the physical world to be unreal and only the world of mind and spirit to be real. To achieve moksha, they seek inner peace and harmony in their lives. Hindus believe that all their actions and deeds will have some future effect—either in this life, or in a future life of their souls. This idea is called the law of karma, and it governs Hindu actions.

Because all human efforts and deeds are subject to the law of karma, Hindus try to erase their desires to achieve something in this utilitarian material world. This is because if they focus on achieving something in this material world, they will only prepare themselves for additional rebirths or new lives (samsara) in future generations on earth. Such efforts never lead to release from the material existence of this world. Moksha cannot be achieved by action aimed at gaining something in this world but only by an experience of oneself as united with god, the oneness of *atman-Brahman*, the union of one's self with the Ultimate Reality.

As we shall see, Hinduism celebrates sacred human fertility and spiritual and creative power. Gradually, it blossoms into the symbolism of the sacred space of the temple and sensuous worship. Finally, Hinduism thrives, united by its believers' faith that there will come a time for a joining with the Ultimate Reality.

CHAPTER 2

The Roots
of Hinduism

*H*induism was not always the complex religion it is today. It developed gradually, as a merging of beliefs and practices of two main groups—the people of the Indus Valley in India and the Aryans of Persia. These groups were not actually Hindus. There was no such thing as Hinduism when they existed. Rather, Hinduism developed from their religious practices, literature, and systems for social order.

Our knowledge of the early stages of Hinduism comes chiefly from archaeological findings and the earliest Hindu scriptures, the *Vedas*. Archaeological artifacts help us to know about the civilization of the Indus Valley, both before and after the Aryan invasion. They tell about practical matters, but they also tell about spiritual life. Scriptures are the center of the beliefs, rituals, and gods of the early Hindus, and they also add to the history of the civilization.

From historical evidence, we know that in this period, early Hindu religious ideas were developed and clarified. Religion was a central part of life in the Indus Valley, and it helped to define the structure of society—the way individuals acted and interacted.

Many of these ideas, both social and religious, still form a part of the basis of Hinduism.

Indus Valley Civilization

About five thousand years ago, in what is today Pakistan and northwestern India, a lively culture flourished on the banks of the Indus River. The Indus people lived in brick houses in well-planned villages. They were successful food cultivators who raised buffalos, goats, sheep, pigs, and dogs. They also exported cotton. Their comfortable civilization was built on a thriving agricultural and animal economy.

The Indus were governed by a strong ruling class who had much concern for cleanliness, order, and stability. As we know from archaeological findings, personal hygiene and ritual cleanliness were of special importance to the Indus. Each house in an Indus valley village had a bathing room with drains. Also, there are many remains of bathing areas located in public places.

In one of the major Indus towns, Mohenjo-Daro, was the Great Bath, a principal public structure. It contained a large water tank with entry steps leading downward at each end. Special rooms for private bathing surrounded the tank. Such rooms and a large water tank are still a common feature of modern Hindu temples.

Most information about the religious life of the Indus Valley people comes from the artifacts they have left behind. These include numerous terra-cotta figurines and seals such as those found by archaeologists in Mohenjo-Daro and another major town, Harappa. These relics provide information about the beliefs of the Indus people as well as their craftsmanship. We know from the seals and figurines that the Indus people honored fertility, sexual power, and certain sacred animals.

It is not certain how the seals from Harappa and Mohenjo-Daro were used. Many of the scenes depicted on the seals relate to the sacredness of sexual power and human creativity. Some scholars have indicated that whatever their use, the seals serve as evidence of the high quality of work produced by the two towns.

The terra-cotta figurines are so numerous that they seem to have been kept in nearly every home. Their craftsmanship is

■ This drawing shows
the elaborate headdress
of an Indus Valley terra-
cotta figurine.

often rather crude as compared to the seals and some other small-scale sculptures found in the Indus Valley. Because they are somewhat unrefined, the figurines may have been created by the common people for their own use, rather than by expert craftsmen for use by the upper classes.

The most common types of figurines from this period represent what are often considered to be "mother-goddesses." Almost all of these figures convey some idea of fertility and motherhood. They feature a female with wide hips, small breasts, tubular limbs, abundant jewelry, and an elaborate headdress. In some instances, a small child appears on the hip or at the breast. In others, a bulging abdomen suggests pregnancy.

The inspiration for these figures may have been awe and reverence for motherhood, fertility, and the continuity of life. Such sentiments would not have been unusual within early agri-

■ A fertility figurine similar to those excavated at the Indus Valley. Such figurines are called "mother goddesses." A typical Indus Valley goddess has an elaborate headdress and tubular limbs.

cultural societies like that of the Indus Valley—the survival and well-being of these people depended on the bountiful gifts of nature. Therefore, early religious attention in the Indus Valley may have centered around fertility goddesses.

Other objects recovered from Harappa also support the idea that human sexual power and procreation were especially sacred to the people of the Indus Valley. Some, for example, depict bulls and various animals or female figures engaged in some sacred rite. The bull is believed to be a symbol of virility and sexual power. It is a motif commonly depicted in Indus Valley art; out of more than two thousand terra-cotta seals and seal impressions that have been found at the various archaeological sites, bulls predominate over other figures.

It seems that the Indus people considered the human figure to be inappropriate for expressing the sacredness of sexual power. Instead, animals, which were believed to have more strength and vitality than humans, were raised to a sacred status in Indus art works. The celebrations of their sexual fertility likewise stood for human sexuality.

Although not all the animals depicted on the seals were considered sacred, the importance of the bull continues in later Hindu mythology, where it is associated with an important Hindu god, Shiva. Shiva is a fertility god, the lord of beasts, who was sometimes depicted with three faces.

One of the most striking sacred seals of the Harappan culture depicts a horned god who strongly resembles Shiva. On the Harappan seals, this god is seated in a very formal posture—perhaps a posture of meditation—with the soles of his feet pressed together. His arms extend away from the body, his thumbs rest on his knees, and the other fingers point downward. He wears elaborate ornaments and a peculiar headdress consisting of a pair of buffalo horns with a plantlike object between them. Around him are four wild animals—an elephant, a tiger, a rhinoceros, and a buffalo—and beneath his stool are two deer. The surrounding animals and the plantlike growth on his head indicate that he is a fertility god. To the right and left of the head are small protuberances that are believed to represent second and third faces, like those of Shiva's.

■ *Three views of a seal with the bull design. Thousands of such seals have been excavated. The majority of these seals depict bulls, powerful symbols of power and virility.*

■ *A man is shown traveling with his portable linga-shrine. The abstract form of the male and female generative powers has been sacred from the time of the Indus Valley culture. Here, such an image, along with other religious paraphernalia, is being carried for the people on the roadside to worship.*

From the artifacts of the Indus Valley, we gain some insight into the lifestyle and sacred beliefs that would begin to form the basis of Hinduism. We also know that the civilization of the Indus Valley was peaceful, and that it continued uninterrupted for more than one thousand years. This stability of Indus culture was due in part to the inner strength of its peoples and their ability to accept new ideas.

We do not know why the Indus civilization collapsed after such a long, peaceful, and comfortable period. As two possible causes, scholars look to climatic changes and the changing course of the Indus River and its tributaries. The coming of the Aryan invaders from the steppes of eastern Europe through Persia, coud be another important cause.

The Invasion of the Aryans (Indo-Europeans)

The Aryans were one of the many Indo-European tribes that migrated outward from the steppes of eastern Europe. Some of the Aryan tribes journeyed across the mountains of Afghanistan into Pakistan and northwest India. There, more than four thousand years ago, they confronted the Indus Valley civilization.

The Aryans were semi-nomadic warriors who came to Pakistan and northwest India in two-wheeled, horse-drawn chariots. They brought a culture that sharply contrasted with that of the Indus people; the Aryans were skilled in bronze metal work, and had no interest in well-planned, fortified towns or agriculture or cattle raising. Although there is no evidence of Aryan architecture or of any art of quality and complexity, students of ancient civilization have excavated skillfully crafted metal weapons produced by this society.

Aryan literature was largely composed after the Aryans had settled in the Indus Valley. This literature clearly reflects the time when the Aryans confronted the Indus people. Some of their stories, for example, portray victories over a people called *dasas*— god-hating people addicted to strange religious rites.

The Aryans were patriarchal—they worshiped male gods. Goddess worship was unknown to them. Their major deities were gods who had links to the sun, like Indra, Varuna, and Agni. Aryan priests were poets who composed hymns in praise of their gods. Their hymns were intended to be sung during fire sacrifices made to appease the gods of the skies, the middle region, and the earth.

By the time the Aryans arrived in the Indus Valley, the Indus culture in the valley was showing increasing signs of disorder. However, the Aryans did not enter a decayed cultural world. Many important religious elements, such as the reverence toward the Indus mother-goddess, control over sexual power, and ritual cleanliness, persisted in Indus village cultures.

At first, the Aryans ignored non-Aryan religious traditions. Later, however, they adopted some of the elements of Indus religions—those that their own religion could accommodate. Thus the Indus people and their beliefs gradually merged with the Aryan culture. The resulting culture was Aryan in structure, but it incorporated many local and non-Aryan beliefs and practices.

The Vedas and the Vedic Period

The *Vedas* were created by the Aryans who migrated towards north-west India from Persia. Like Hinduism itself, these holy scriptures have acquired many cultural and chronological layers.

Some Vedic thoughts are so old that they reflect an Iranian origin that predates the migration of the Aryans to India in 1500 B.C.E. Other ideas in the *Vedas* evolved while Aryans lived in the Indus Valley. The content of these older texts was absorbed by the Aryans when they came to dominate the different cultures of the Indus Valley. There are four *Vedas*, the oldest and primary scriptures of Hinduism. The *Vedas* provide much historical, sociological, religious, and linguistic information about the people who composed them. They also provide a foundation for many Hindu religious concepts.

The word *veda* means "knowledge." The knowledge that the *Vedas* contain was considered to be of divine origin, revealed by the creator-god Brahman to a group of inspired sages. These sages, or *rishis*, were given the responsibility of transmitting the divine gift to humankind.

For centuries, the *Vedas* were passed by teachers to students through an oral tradition. Even when an alphabet was introduced, there was strong opposition to committing the *Vedas* to writing. The Brahmins (priests) believed that the power of the holy Vedic hymns lay in the tradition of hearing the text, thus the name for such hymns—*shruti* "that which is heard." Memorizing the *Vedas* from written words, according to the Brahmins, brought one no great religious strength. Eventually, however, for the sake of preservation, these holy hymns were written in an old form of Sanskrit that we now call *Vedic*.

In all, there are four *Vedas*. The *Rig Veda* is by far the oldest collection of hymns. Although a precise date for its origin is impossible to pinpoint, scholars estimate the range from 5000 B.C.E. to 900 B.C.E. The present written text can be estimated to have existed by at least 300 B.C.E.

The *Rig Veda* contains hymns and praises to the gods. The second *Veda*, composed around 700 B.C.E., is called the *Yajur Veda*. It contains a variation of the *Rig Veda* text. In addition, it provides details for performing sacrifices, building altars, and reciting ritual phrases. In essence, it is the Brahmins' handbook.

The two remaining *Vedas*—*Sama Veda* and *Atharva Veda*—contain significant portions of the *Rig Veda*, and both offer supplementary guidelines for priestly behavior. However, some differences do exist between these two *Vedas*. Parts of the *Sama Veda*, for example, center on sacrifices to Soma, a god of enthusiasm and intoxication whose worship developed from an undiscovered stimulant akin to the intoxication brought on by certain wild mushrooms. The hymns of the *Atharva Veda* are more concerned with magic spells, charms, and incantations. These fall into one of two categories: those of a healing, medicinal nature, such as love potions, cure-alls, and blessings; and those of a negative character, calling down misfortune or sickness upon enemies.

Early Vedic religion centered around divine power. The gods, called *devas*, comprised a pantheon (community) of divine powers. The number of the gods was not important—rather, the functions of the gods, or the way they were associated with natural events or phenomena were important. Devas were classified as celestial, atmospheric, or terrestrial, depending on the primary location of their activity: sky; atmospheric region, and earth.

Celestial Gods

The Vedic people believed in many celestial gods: *Varuna*, the guardian of cosmic law; *Mitra*, Varuna's chief assistant and a friend and benefactor of humankind; *Surya*, who represented the physical aspect of the sun; and *Savitri*, who represented the sun's ability to stimulate life.

To invite the celestial gods down to earth, into their special places of prayer and worship, the early Hindus performed rituals. The god was honored with an offering of food and hymns of praise. A typical sacrificial hymn contained an invocation, or calling, to the god, offered in a tone of friendliness, reverence, or fear—depending on the god and one's relation to the god. The following is one such Vedic hymn, offered to the sky god Varuna:

> *Forgive, O gracious Lord, forgive! Whatever sin we*
> *mortals have committed against the people of the gods,*
> *if, foolish, we have thwarted your decrees, O god,*
> *do not destroy us in your anger!*   (Basham 240)

Varuna was one of the most important gods of the early Vedic period. He was the overseer of moral action, and his guidance was the standard for cosmic, moral, and religious order. This order is called *rita.* Varuna created the world and ruled it by the standard of rita. Rita also provided a structure for other celestial devas.

Vishnu was a minor celestial god during the early Vedic period. Later, Vishnu would become one of the three major gods of Hinduism. His main distinction in the *Vedas* was the three strides by which he crossed the earth, the atmosphere, and then reached "the highest place," his special heaven. This ability was a significant factor in his later rise to prominence.

Atmospheric Gods

Hindus of the early Vedic period also believed in another class of *devas* (gods). These were the atmospheric gods who included Indra, the god of lightning and thunder, *Vayu,* the god of wind, the *Maruts,* a troop of storm gods, and *Rudra,* the father of the Maruts.

Indra, a model warrior, was a figure of great popularity and prestige. In fact, he was the second most important god of the early Vedic era. The key to his character was a myth describing his conquest of the demon *Vritra,* a serpentine monster who blocked the flow of life-giving waters to the Aryans. It is said that Indra not only slew this mythic enemy—he also fought the real enemies of the Aryans, the *dasas,* or slaves, of the Indus Valley. Indra is called the Fortress Splitter and is praised for his destruction of the fortified citadels of Aryan opponents. With his belly full of exhilarating drink and his thunderbolt ready, Indra represented what an Aryan warrior aspired to be.

Rudra, the father of the Maruts, or storm gods, was feared because of his malevolent and destructive nature. He was also praised at times for his ability to protect his people from misfortune by sending storms upon their enemies. Rudra was a minor deva, far overshadowed by Varuna and Indra during this early Vedic period. In later Hinduism, however, his characteristics merged with the qualities of a non-Aryan, Indus Valley deity—an early form of the god Shiva. He then became one of the three major Hindu gods.

CHAPTER 3

The Late Vedic Period and the Upanishadic Period

*A*round the ninth century B.C.E., Aryan tribes migrated slowly across the plains of northern India to the Ganges Valley. By about the end of the seventh century B.C.E., Aryans as well as non-Aryans occupied the Ganges valley. They were organized into distinct principalities, or states. Some were ruled by hereditary rulers called *rajahs*. Others, who were still in community groups of largely non-Aryan clans, were governed by chieftains. The principalities were populated by people of various ethnic compositions. There were light-skinned Aryans, dark-skinned Indus Valley people, and local tribal people of the Ganges valley who had distinct skin coloration.

In the areas they occupied, the Aryans formed the upper strata of a still-fluid social order. Below them were the non-Aryans. This separation among the classes was not hard and fast. However, the Brahmins, or priests, distinguished four classes of people: *Brahmins*, the priests; the ruling *Rajanyas* or *Shatriyas* who, for the most part, were warriors; the *Vaishyas*, or common people such as artisans and farmers; and the *Shudras*, servants who are thought to have been non-Aryan natives.

The belief in separate classes, the *caste system*, was supported and given religious sanction by a hymn in the Vedic scripture.

In the late Vedic period, the Aryans' world view gradually changed. Major gods of the early Vedic period lost their importance. In later Vedic writings, interest shifted away from celestial and atmospheric gods toward devas who were located on the land. Also, more attention was directed toward sacrificial rituals.

It was during this period that the Brahmins, or priests, gained importance and power in early Hindu society. Eventually, people came to question the Brahmins' role. The period following the Vedic period, the already mentioned era of the Upanishads, showed the results of this questioning.

Through the Upanishadic era, we see that the religious history of the Hindus was never static. There had been a dynamic process of growth and innovation throughout the early period. From the hymns of the *Vedas* to the compilations of the *Brahmanas* and the *Aranyakas* (the forest books), there was a constant growth that followed the changing times of the society. The Upanishadic period was vibrant with new ideas, speculation, and knowledge. The rejection of beliefs with which people could not identify and the quest for new answers filled the teachings of the *Upanishads* and inspired new schools of thought.

Terrestrial Gods and the Importance of Sacrifice

Sacrifice became an important part of Hindu life in the late Vedic period. As a result, only gods directly associated with sacrifices—such as *Agni*, the god of fire, *Soma*, the god of sacrificial libation or the pouring drinks, and *Brahaspati*, the divine priest and lord of prayer—retained the interest of the later Vedic priests. In this later era, Varuna, Indra, and others only received minor sacrifices.

During this era, the religious life of the Hindus became increasingly dominated by the rituals performed around a fire pit. These so-called "fire-sacrifice" rituals gradually became very complex. Fire was now believed to be the creative source of all the powers of the gods and of nature. Fire rituals were of two kinds: *griha*, domestic rituals performed by the householder or priests, and *shrauta*, specialized rites performed by priests for patrons who paid for the sacrifice.

In *shrauta* rituals, Vedic hymns were recited by the Brahmin. The *shrauta* sacrifices were complicated, and over time, they became more and more elaborate and complex. Sacrificial duties, then, had to be divided among several priests. Performing the sacrifice, once meant to be a celebration of the devas, gradually came to be viewed as bringing power in its own right. Thus priests came to hold a lot of power in Hindu society.

While rites performed by priests became more complicated, *griha*, or domestic rites, remained simple. They celebrated the new and full moons, the seasons of the year, and the first fruit of the harvest, or they marked special family occasions such as the building of a new house, the birth of a son, and the passage through important stages of life. *Griha* rites could be performed on a household fire maintained by a pious parent, following the rituals spelled out over the years by the priests.

Gradually, the distinction between the *shrauta* and *griha* rituals became obscured, because both types of rites were subject to priestly influence and control. Even though *griha* rituals could be performed at home, they were still taught by priests and controlled

■ *Two priests performing the* **shrauta** *ritual using* **Agni** — *the god of fire — as the central element.*

by priests. Interestingly, most domestic rituals have been handed down from Vedic times to the present with little change or elaboration. Today, however, priests do not control the *griha* rituals.

During fire sacrifices, people offered their possessions to the gods. The most important sacrificial offerings were placed in a fire. People believed that the god Agni conveyed their offerings to the other gods through the fire. Agni was thought to be both the god of fire and the sacrificial fire itself. As the god of fire, he was the medium through which humans could relate to the other gods:

> *You, O Agni, are Indra, the bull of all that exists;*
> *You are the wide striding Vishnu, worthy of reverence;*
> *O Lord of the Holy Word (Brahaspati),*
> *you are the chief priest.*
>
> *. . . You, O Agni, are King Varuna, whose laws are firm;*
> *You are Mitra, the wonder-worker to be revered . . .*
> *You, O Agni, are Rudra, the Asura of lofty heaven;*
> *As the troops of Maruts, you control sustenance.*
> *(Rig Veda II.1, 3, 4, 6 Hopkins 18)*

In sacrifices, Agni represented all the other gods. As the messenger to them, Agni linked humankind to the divine world. Because he could assume various forms of fire, Agni was believed to be an example of the divine world throughout nature.

Agni quickly became an all important deity. In the celestial region, Agni was the sun. In the atmospheric region, he was lightning. Finally, by lightning he was brought to the earth, and rekindled as fire from the trees in which he was hidden. When *shrauta* rituals were performed, three kinds of fire were kept so that they might symbolically represent Agni of the sky, of the atmosphere, and of the earth.

In the late Vedic period, other sacrificial elements also grew in importance. In particular, the element of sound and the sacred actions accompanying repetitive sound became essential to the sacrifice. During the offering of sacrifices, ritual statements called *mantras*, or verse-prayers, were recited. Mantras were thought to capture the power of Brahman, the Upanishadic Ultimate Reality.

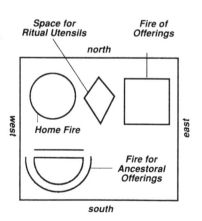

■ Diagram of a sacrificial plot used for the **Shrauta** ritual.

Because of its deep wisdom, and often because of its magical power, the mantras or the sacred speech soon became more important to know than the natural world. Eventually, sacred speech was deified in the form of the goddess *Vac* (meaning "speech").

The gods themselves are said to have performed sacrifices to obtain their places in the Vedic heaven. Although the early *Vedas* are not known for stories of creation, by the end of the oldest and most important *Veda*, the *Rig Veda*, such a story had developed. The story told of a god known as Prajapati, the lord of beings, who was also known as Purusha. It was believed that he existed before the foundation of the universe. Prajapati was a primeval human being who was sacrificed by the gods who were his children. From the body of this divine victim, the universe was created. The "Hymn of the Primeval Man," from the *Rig Veda*, describes this first cosmic sacrifice that brought forth the universe:

> When the gods made a sacrifice with the Man (Purusha)
> as their victim, Spring was the melted butter, summer
> the fuel, and Autumn the oblation. From that all-
> embracing sacrifice the clotted butter was collected.
> From it he made the animal of air and wood and village.
> From that all-embracing sacrifice were born the hymns
> and chants, from that the meters were born, from that
> the sacrificial spells were born. Thence were born horses,
> and all beings with two rows of teeth. Thence were born
> cattle, and thence goats and sheep. When they divided
> the Man, into how many parts did they divide him?
> What was his mouth, what were his arms, what were
> his thighs and his feet called? The Brahmin was his
> mouth, of his arms was made the Kshatriya, his thighs
> became the Vaishya, or his feet the Shudra was born. The
> moon arose from his mind. From his eye was born the
> sun. From his mouth Indra and Agni. From his breath
> the wind was born From his navel came the air From
> his head there came the sky, from his feet the earth, the
> four quarters from his ear, Thus they fashioned the
> world. With Sacrifice the gods sacrificed to sacrifice.

These were the first of the sacred laws. The mighty
beings reached the sky, where are the eternal spirits,
the gods. (Basham 242-43)

In this poem, parallels are made between Purusha's sacrificed body and all the levels of creation. All creation is given a religious association in which Purusha, the cosmic victim, is centrally important. The cosmos, the world of nature, human society, and sacrifice are seen as similar and parallel, all created at the same time for all ages by Purusha's sacrifice.

According to the poem, the sacrifice of Purusha, the cosmic victim, is the reference point for all things. His sacrifice is the key to creation. Early Hindus believed that all other sacrifices were imitations of this great sacrifice. Furthermore, they also believed that to know Purusha's sacrifice was to know the universe.

Brahmins and Power

Throughout much of the Vedic period, the Brahmins (priests) held a central place of power in society. This was in part because the Brahmins controlled and oversaw the sacrifices in which the gods came down to earth to partake in offerings by their devotees. As mentioned, these included shrauta and griha rituals. The Brahmins also held additional power because they controlled knowledge of the *Vedas.*

The *Vedas* were passed from teacher to student in the oral tradition. They had to be studied and memorized by priests, and then told to members of other castes. Because of this, members of the priestly caste could literally hold the knowledge within their caste. Brahmins not only knew the sacrificial hymns and prayers by heart, but they were considered to be the only specialists qualified to perform the holy fire sacrifices for the people. Thus the Brahmins controlled common access to the gods and ultimately to the entire cosmos.

By the end of the Vedic period, the Brahmins had made a supplementary addition to each of the four *Vedas.* These four compilations were called *Brahmanas.* They contained guidance for priests in the use of hymns and prayers. The *Brahmanas* gave practical directions, in exhaustive detail, for carrying out all types of sacrifice.

To explain the deeper meaning of these complex rites, still more explanations had to be compiled. These further explanations were known as *Aranyakas*, or forest books, because the teaching of them took place in forest retreats. Although the *Brahmanas* insisted on proper ritual actions, the *Aranyakas* seemed to claim that the understanding of the meaning behind the ritual actions was more important. They claimed that perfect ritual did not depend on elaborate fire sacrifices but could be performed within one's own mind. The compilation of the *Brahmanas* and *Aranyakas* clearly shows how fascinated and absorbed the Vedic priests were with their rituals and the process of elaborating on them and interpreting them.

The use of the *Brahmanas'* rituals was limited to those who were considered to be ritually pure and fit. A knowledge of the proper ritual actions brought people offering sacrifices into the company of those having direct access to the gods. If the rituals were properly performed by the priests throughout their lives, it was believed that after death, both the priests and those who asked them to offer the sacrifices would be rewarded with an existence freed from their mortal bodies. In short, they would be elevated to the world of the gods.

Over time, many people became disenchanted with the complex rituals mandated by the Brahmins. Also, the idea that the universe was formed and maintained through Purusha's sacrifice lost religious support. Different ideas about the world's creation and life's meaning gained attention.

One widely believed theory stated that the world could be explained in terms of a neutral, or impersonal, principle. This principle was known simply as "that One." The following hymn contains an alternative explanation for the creation of the universe. It clearly questions the early Vedic vision of creation:

> *Then there were neither death nor immortality,*
> *Nor was there then the torch of night and day*
> *The one breathed windlessly and self-sustaining*
> *There was that One then, and there was no other*
> *At first there was only darkness wrapped in darkness*
> *All this was only unillumined water*
> *That one which came to be, enclosed in nothing,*

Arose at last, born of the power of heat (Tapas)
In the beginning desire (Kama, creative or
sacrificial impulse) descended on it—
that was the primal seed, born of the mind . . .
But, after all, who knows, and who can say
Whence it all came, and how creation happened?
The gods themselves are later than creation,
So who knows truly whence it has arisen?
Whence all creation had its origin,
He, whether he fashioned it or whether he did not,
He, who surveys it all from highest heaven,
He knows, or perchance he knows not.
(Rig Veda X.129.6,7)

As a result of spiritual and social questioning, a way of life quite in contrast to all the complex rituals of the Brahmins became increasingly common at this time. This was the lifestyle of people known as *ascetics*. Ascetics are dedicated to great austerity and self-discipline in their lives. In late Vedic times, they tended to live as hermits in the forest and chose not to participate in the Hindu social structure with its many castes.

Ascetics emerged from all sections of society and rivaled the Brahmins, or priests, in commanding the highest respect of the people. The passion that fueled the austere devotion of the ascetic in the forest was itself revered as sacrificial; this passionate dedication to the austere life was compared to a fire on the altar. The repetition of Vedic chants that characterized the lives of the Vedic priests was thought to be equivalent to the austere devotion of these ascetics. The heat of such ascetic devotion and prayer was called *tapas,* or the heat of knowledge. The simple and sincere acts of the ascetics were thought to bring a higher understanding of the Ultimate Reality. Indeed, it allowed the ascetics to have a higher understanding of all reality.

The ascetics, or forest hermits, were also adept in various forms of meditation, or quiet thinking. Some were called *munis* (silent ones) and others, *rishis* (having the power of knowledge). The *munis* were described as those who ". . . wear the wind as a girdle, and who are drunk with their own silence. They know the thoughts of all the people, for they have drunk the magic cup of Rudra/Shiva, which is poison to ordinary mortals."

Because ascetics led lives of austerity and purity, it was believed that they could generate "the heat of deep knowledge" by their acts of meditation and by their ascetic practices. People began to believe more and more that without priests, they themselves could experience the power of meditation and ascetic practice to bring on deep religious knowledge. Meditation and asceticism were seen as keys to religious fervor, and they were available to forest hermits as well as to those who wanted to imitate their activities.

The religious example of the ascetics presented an alternative religious form of life for many people. The Vedic tradition of the Brahmins seemed centered on the priests and the exact performance of their rituals. Having become, to some degree, disenchanted with the elaborate sacrifices of the Brahmins, many people wanted to know if there was some higher goal to life than offering exactly performed sacrifices. People began to search for a state of immortality, a life not ruled by death and not eroded by time. They also wondered how such a state could be obtained—how they might transcend or overcome the defeating condition of a life where there seemed to be no hope of something greater. The Upanishadic period tried to answer some of these new religious questions.

The Upanishadic Period

The Upanishadic period (800-450 B.C.E.) was one of the greatest eras of creative thinking in the history of Hinduism. During this period, people took a more questioning attitude toward human existence. Upanishadic ascetics were philosophers, teachers, and seers. They lived in forest hermitages. They spent their days studying, contemplating, and discussing the puzzling questions of the universe. Young minds were attracted to these hermitages, hoping to engage in debates there and thus find enlightenment.

The *Upanishads* were composed by these forest hermits around 700-500 B.C.E., as the last section of the *Vedas*. They are also known as shruti, or "listened to" texts, and almost all of their

■ *An* **Upanishadic** *sage/philosopher in a forest hermitage discusses the meaning of life and the nature of reality with his student.*

teachings are in the form of dialogues. The meaning of the word *Upanishad* is "sitting down near" a guru (spiritual master) who passes on his secret teachings. More than one hundred compilations of these dialogues are written down, though only thirteen of them are accepted as smriti, or sacred scriptures. Generally, the *Upanishads* discuss the relationship between the individual and the universe, the nature of the universal soul, the meaning of life, and the character of life after death.

The Upanishadic period introduced to Hinduism a new and influential kind of thinking and questioning. In principle, these texts differed from the *Vedas* in that they did not exclude people outside the Brahmin caste. However, the content of the *Upanishads* is subtle and profound. Since understanding the *Upanishadic* concepts has been considered a difficult task, only a few, in fact, come to deep knowledge of their teachings.

Despite the complexity of the *Upanishads*, men and women of all classes participated in Upanishadic learning. It was not one's class or caste but one's character that was important. Honesty, for example, was much more highly valued in a potential student to a hermitage than was a person's family tree.

One passage from the *Upanishads* poignantly expresses how much the inner person was appreciated within this religious community:

Satyakama was the son of a woman named Jabala.
One day her son asked, "Mother, I want to be a student.
What is my family name?" His mother replied, "My dear,
I don't know your family. I had you when I was very
young traveling as a servant. My name is Jabala, and
yours is Satyakama, so you are Satyakama Jabala."
The next day the boy went to a teacher by the name of
Gautama Haridrumata, and said: "I want to be your
student, sir. Can I?" The teacher asked what his family
name was. Satyakama replied, "I don't know my family,
sir. I asked my mother and she said that she had me in
her youth, when she traveled about a lot as a servant . . .
She said she was Jabala and I was Satyakama and that
I was to give my name as Satyakama Jabala." The
teacher replied, "Nobody but a true brahman would be
so honest!" He said, "Go and fetch me fuel, my friend,
and I will initiate you, for you have not swerved
from the truth."

Two of the oldest (circa 700-500 B.C.E.) and most significant of the Upanishadic scriptures are the *Brihadaranyaka Upanishad* and the *Chandayoga Upanishad*. In the *Chandayoga Upanishad,* a question is posed so that its answer can show the relationship between the sacrificial fire on the altar, the fire in the sun, and tapas (the heat of understanding). The question is about the creative powers in the universe. It is formulated in this way: What is the nature of the One that is the cause of the whole of existence? The answer discusses the creative powers of tapas, of sacrifice, and of the ultimate truth, Brahman.

Students of the *Upanishads* believed that it was not the ritual acts of sacrifices themselves, but rather the spirit behind the sacrifices that was important. They believed that through meditation or reflection they could attain the knowledge of how they were related to the gods, and how this divine link originated. They also wanted to know what were their real selves and what was the relationship of their real selves to the Universal Reality, that is, Brahman.

Such spiritual reflection and searching was believed to cause tapas (the heat of knowledge) within the dedicated student. By setting aside all other concerns, the student really was "sacrificing" them. In this respect, these individuals set aside or "sacrificed" worldly concerns and thereby performed sacrifices on the altar of their hearts. Such self-sacrifices paralleled the fire sacrifices of the Vedic priests.

Upanishadic ascetics sacrificed their selves, disciplined their bodily concerns, and desired enlightenment. They believed that this showed a power to transcend worldly cares and contemplate the important questions of reality. Such practices led to a belief that an individual had, beyond a surface self, an essential or real self. The question, then, was to ask what this essential self was and how one could grasp it. This question, which is still important in modern Hinduism, was answered in part by a new idea of the Ultimate.

In the *Upanishads*, all the many gods of the Vedic tradition are reduced to one, Brahman. Brahman was believed to be the supreme essence of the universe. This essence is seen in the universe, in the various creations of the physical world, and in the soul of individuals.

A major focus of the Upanishadic thinkers was the idea that an individual's soul, called *atman*, was a separate part of Brahman, or the universal soul. Since the Upanishadic era, Hindus have believed that atman, the individual soul, *is* Brahman, the universal soul. It has been separated as atman but after achieving *moksha* or salvation, it will be united again with Brahman. Eventually, the word *Brahman* was used to refer to the universal essence containing all kinds of power.

The idea of *atman-Brahman* is repeated in the famous phrase from the *Chandayoga Upanishad*, "tat tvam asi," literally, "that thou art." This phrase means that there is no difference between the individual and the universal. A story from the *Chandayoga Upanishad* well illustrates this connection:

> *Svetaketu asked his father-teacher to make him*
> *understand what Atman and Brahman were.*

Father said, "Fetch me a fruit of the banyan tree."
"Here is one, sir." "What do you see?" "Very tiny
seeds, sir." "Break one." "I have broken it, sir."
"Now what do you see?" "Nothing, sir." "My son,"
the father said, "what you do not perceive is the
essence, and in that essence the mighty banyan
tree exists. Believe me, my son, in that essence is the
Self of all that is. That is the True, that is the Self.
Tat tvam asi. And you are that Self, Svetaketu."

In this story, the soul is depicted as the innermost or the real self. This innermost self is in no sense a physical thing. The identity of the soul of the individual and the soul of the universe is the central theme throughout the Upanishadic texts. *Tat tvam asi*, "you (the individual soul) are that (the universal essence) is the principal teaching of the period. Another story illustrating this truth is found in the *Brhadaranyaka Upanishad*:

"Put this salt in water, and come to me in the morning."
The student did as he was told. In the morning the teacher
said, "Fetch the salt." The student looked for it, but could
not find it, because it had dissolved. "Taste the water
from the top," said the teacher. "How does it taste?"
"Of salt," the student replied. 'Taste from the middle.
How does it taste?" "Of salt," the student replied.
"Taste from the bottom. How does it taste?" "Of salt"
the student answered. Then the teacher said, "You
don't perceive that one Reality exists in your own body,
my dear, but it is truly there. Everything which has
its being in that subtle essence. That is Reality!
That is the Soul! And you are that, Svetaketu!"

Samsara, Karma, and Moksha

Of the many Upanishadic teachings that were to become permanent elements of Hinduism, those of *samsara* and karma are the most prominent. By the time of the *Upanishads*, many Hindus considered that the everyday world, brought forth and maintained by gods, might be a trap in which people could be caught up in continuing cycles of birth, death, and rebirth. Conceivably, this could go on forever. The concept of *samsara* gave some hope that one might improve one's condition.

Samsara is a belief in the transmigration, or continual passing, of a soul from one body to another. It can be described as follows. The soul of a person who dies does not pass into heaven, or hell, or elsewhere. It is reborn into another body, which may be of higher or lower order than one's previous existence. Rebirth follows rebirth in an endless chain. Thus, a person of low status may be reborn as a priest, or a king, or an animal, or even a worm. The question then arises: What causes the soul to enter a higher or lower state of existence?

A person's higher or lower state of existence is determined by the law of karma (the law of deeds or works.) This is a law determining that an individual's thoughts, words, and deeds have ethical consequences that establish the quality of their future existences. For Hindus, the law of karma is a necessary law of nature. It decides the quality of a Hindu's further life. A person who has done good deeds is reborn into a good existence in the next birth, and if he has done bad deeds, had evil thoughts, and spoken bad words, he is reborn as an animal.

Karma does not only apply to one's future life; it also applies to what happens in one's present life. According to the law of Karma, the good that a person does in this life eventually comes back to him in the form of good fortune, either in one's present life or in one's future existence. Likewise, a person pays a "karmic price" for the evil deeds he might have performed. His evil deed will come back to "haunt" him in this present life or in his future existence.

The highest of the Upanishadic teachings completes the ideas of samsara and karma. This is the concept of moksha, or release: by leading a good spiritual life, that is, by union with Brahman, or the Ultimate Reality, an individual will eventually leave the temporary existences and the cycle of samsara. With the idea of moksha, the desire for eternal oneness with Brahman became more important than improving one's position in this life or gaining physical enjoyment by good deeds or karma.

In the Upanishadic era, Hindus gradually placed an increasingly higher value on the goal of union with the Universal Soul

■ A **yogi** can be recognized by his matted, tangled hair. He has no possessions. He wears a loose cloak and carries with him a wooden staff and a flute. He has renounced his social status in order to find the highest truth (**Brahman**) through mental and physical discipline. His goal is to be spiritually united with **Brahman** in order to achieve salvation, **moksha**.

and release from the realm of samsara. Moksha came to be considered the highest and perhaps the sole purpose of life. Over the years, various Hindu sects strived toward this same goal, but they did so through different methods.

Along with the new ideas of sacrifice, god, and the cycle of samsara, the Upanishadic period also saw many new schools of religious philosophy. One of these was yoga. Yoga is a form of physical and mental discipline. Although its practice was much older than the *Upanishads*, the common methods of yoga were further developed and explained in this era. Upanishadic seers followed yogic techniques which emphasized the difference between the body and the self.

Those who practiced yoga believed that it could lead them to a state in which atman became one with Brahman. This was possible because the self in its deepest reality was believed already to be like Brahman—pure, limitless, and unchanging. People who practiced yoga and had this special experience of union with Brahman were called *jivanmukta* (those who are liberated while still alive).

Vedanta was another powerful school of religious philosophy that emerged at this time. It fostered the idea that there was an underlying unity to all reality. It introduced the concept of *maya*, an impersonal force that makes people forget that all individuals are part of the universal essence. Maya is believed to be the cause of all ignorance and suffering and must be overcome.

New Methods of Teaching

The instruction of the *Upanishads* promised a religious teaching that would be centered on ordinary people and not on the detailed sacrificial rites of the Brahmins. However, many common people had difficulty understanding the texts. The Upanishadic teachings were simply too philosophical and puzzling. During the same time as the Upanishadic period, some non-Brahmin thinkers, such as Buddhists and Jains, came to reject the old sacrificial tradition of the Brahmins. These teachers began to convey their religious lessons in new ways—through the telling of stories and parables.

Coming out of the confines of the forest schools that had been the classrooms of the *Upanishads,* the new teachers traveled from one town to the next. While traveling, they told stories and spread their beliefs and ideas. The people listened eagerly and were entranced by the simple parables. They found the teachings uplifting. They also discovered that the stories brought them understanding of their lives and of the world.

Soon the stories and parables, which often illustrated moral or religious lessons, became very popular. Seeing that this approach to religious teaching was successful, even the Brahmins began to adopt storytelling as part of their preaching method. Consequently, new forms of Brahmanic literature came into existence around the third century B.C.E. At that time, the Brahmins wrote new literature as well as additions to older works. Some examples of how the Brahmins adapted the new teaching methods can be seen in the additions they made to the great epic poems, the *Ramayana* and the *Mahabharata,* and also to the sacred writings known as *Puranas.*

Originally, the *Ramayana* and the *Mahabharata* were long, nonreligious stories about the exploits and struggles of warriors and kings, told by generations of traveling bards. Later, all sorts of material was added to these basic stories. So much material was incorporated into the original stories that each of the great epics, especially the *Mahabharata,* developed into an encyclopedia of heroes and legends—some legends giving historical portraits, some creating mythological images. It is in the epics that one encounters the ever-developing characters of the great gods Shiva and Vishnu, their wives, their families, and numerous other minor gods.

Whereas the epics seem to have reached their final form by 500 C.E., the *Puranas* continued to develop until late in the twelfth century C.E. The *Puranas,* or "old stories," incorporate legends, myths, and customary observances. Later portions of the *Puranas* focused on stories of the gods Brahma, Vishnu, and Shiva. Hindus worshiped each of these three gods separately, but the three were also considered to be one god with three functions: creation (Brahma), preservation (Vishnu) and destruction (Shiva).

The myths and legends of the *Puranas* brought meaning to people's lives. Because the legends were often intertwined with significant historical facts, the *Puranas* were often associated with *itihasa* (history). Like the epics, Puranic texts are considered important because they have been, and still are, the media of mass education in the Hindu world. For centuries, religious, social, and cultural norms and inspirations have been imparted through this type of literature.

While many works may bear the name purana, only eighteen are traditionally acknowledged as shruti, or sacred. These are called *Mahapuranas,* "great old stories." It is also true that any religious text could be called a minor purana. Many minor puranas that were written after the older shruti were referred to as *Mahatmyas* or "glorifications." These mostly glorified gods and places of pilgrimage. Among these are *Mahatmyas,* modern religious texts, some composed as recently as the nineteenth century.

CHAPTER **4**

The Gods and Devotionalism

During the period between 500 B.C.E. and 400 C.E., the *Puranas* were inspired by various Hindu sects. Within each sect, individuals considered one god to be their personal god and the highest god. What developed with this more personal religious perspective was a popular devotional movement known as *bhakti*, "attachment," or fervent devotion to a god.

The seeds of this new approach to religion had been sown in the earlier traditions of both the epics and the Puranas. We can see how the seeds developed if we study some of the stories of the gods and the people's new appreciation of certain gods. In the earlier periods, these gods had small roles within the Hindu pantheon. They took on new dimensions and gained in importance as the years moved on.

The Ambiguous God Shiva

Shiva was not a prominent god in the earlier writings of the Brahmins. In the *Vedas*, the forerunner of the god Shiva was the terrible atmospheric deva Rudra, an Aryan god of storms, lightning, and medicinal herbs. Because Rudra controlled atmospheric

forces, the Indus Valley people believed that he could direct human destiny. In return for the prayers of his worshipers, Rudra gave them healing remedies and protected them against the destruction brought by powerful storms.

By the period of the *Upanishads,* Rudra's characteristics merged with those of another Indus Valley terrestrial god of cattle to form Shiva, one of three major gods. He was the Indus yogic god having counsel over sexuality. He was the Vedic god of terrible rains and storm, and the healing god of herbs. In addition, he was the deity of animals, the father of storm gods, and the god of

■ *Preceding page - Rama, Sita, and Lakshamana on their way to the forest after being banished by Rama's stepmother. In this picturesque landscape, they are being served by the forest hermits.*

■ *Shiva is shown here with his wife Parvati and their two sons Skanda and Ganesha. This picture depicts both the benign and the terrible symbols of Shiva. Although the holy family is seated in the middle of a calm and peaceful landscape, the foreground shows a cremation ground with burning pyres and bones from human skeletons.*

yogic power. He became known for his contradictory powers, particularly sexual power and the power of yogic self-control. Religious awe of the complex figure of Shiva and his wife, Parvati, emerged into the tradition of Shiva worship—referred to as Shaivism—during the early decades (third century B.C.E.) of the Puranic time period.

Many myths provide absorbing portraits of Shiva's multi-sided nature. These myths occur often in the epics and the *Puranas*. Each time, the stories are told a bit differently, depending on the storyteller and the time they were written down.

One myth about Shiva tells how the gods were constantly struggling with demons (*raksasas*). To strengthen themselves in their struggle, the gods decided to use *amrita*, the elixir of immortality. To produce this elixir, they had to churn the Ocean of Milk. The gods used the serpent Vasuki as their churning rope. Having been churned around for some time, the serpent vomited forth poison. Just as the poison was about to fall into the elixir, contaminate it, and destroy all hope for the gods, Shiva, the god of gods, came to the rescue. He caught the poison in his mouth and saved the gods' drink of immortality. He himself was saved from swallowing it by his wife Parvati, who strangled him so that the poison would stay in his throat. This is why some portraits of Shiva give him a blue throat.

In the *Mahabharata*, Shiva is not only worshiped as creator of the universe, but also as the primeval father. The great epic tells of Shiva living in the Himalaya Mountains with his wife Parvati (a beneficent and mild form of the great goddess Mahadevi Shakti) and their two sons, Ganesha and Skanda. They also live with Shiva's constant companion and *vahana* ("vehicle") Nandi, the bull–a symbol of male strength and power.

Throughout the Hindu legends, Shiva is depicted in many different forms. A popular form of Shiva is that of the lord of dance, Nataraja. His sacred cosmic dance has the power to remove all evils and obstacles. Nataraja stands in a posture of dance in the middle of a fiery halo. The flaming mandorla represents the universe with all its illusion, suffering, and pain.

Within this universe, the Nataraja dances. The locks of his hair are decked with a crescent moon, a skull, and a tiny symbol of the sacred river Ganges. The skull, with its faint smile, laughs at people who consider themselves eternal, unable to realize how fleeting life is. The crescent moon in his matted hair keeps Kama, the god of nightly love, alive, and through the waxing and waning of the moon he creates different seasons and rejuvenates life. The river Ganges that flows in Nataraja's hair originally flowed in heaven. When the heavenly Ganges was needed on earth, she was unwilling to descend because she realized that her fall from heaven to earth would be too heavy for the earth to withstand. So Shiva, as Nataraja, agreed to break the violent power of the sacred river's fall by catching her in his tangled hair.

Shiva also wears snakes coiled around his upper arms and his neck, symbolizing his control over these most deadly animals. Although snakes are the most dreaded poisonous animals on land, Shiva's power diminishes their terrible nature. Snakes also symbolize the transmigration or change that souls undergo as they inhabit different bodies. Snakes shed their skin in due season and grow a new one—just as in Hindu belief humans obtain a new body with each rebirth of their soul.

In two of his four hands, Shiva often holds a drum and a flame. The drum represents the rhythmic sound to which Nataraja dances and ceaselessly recreates the universe. The flames represent the destructive energy with which Nataraja dances at the end of each cosmic age, cleansing sins and removing illusion. His right hand blesses devotees. His left hand, pointing toward his foot, grants eternal bliss to those who approach him. The other foot treads firmly upon the dwarf of ignorance, allowing the birth of knowledge.

In addition, Shiva's form as Nataraja reveals a tradition that revered the power of female and male sexuality. From his left earlobe hangs a female earring and from his right earlobe a male earring. These symbolize the union of the archetypal parents of the universe.

The worship of sexual power that was prominent in pre-Aryan times had no place in the early Vedic hymns. However, the tradition of reverence for sexual power and the need for self-control was probably carried on for centuries outside the *Vedas* in the Brahmanic tradition. With the emergence in the Puranic texts

The "auspicious" head of Shiva shows a crescent moon, indicating the phases of lunar time. A miniature form of the sacred river Ganges adorns Shiva's matted hair. A smiling skull adorns the front of his headgear, and his dissimilar earrings represent his male and female aspects.

of both Shiva and Shakti—the primeval father and mother—the worship of sexual power resurfaced. And some of the most potent symbols in Hinduism are associated with Shiva as the god of regeneration and sexuality.

In Shaivism, which is the cult of Shiva worship, the central objects of worship are symbols of sexual power. Even the Ultimate Reality of Brahman is often represented by symbolic forms of the genitals, such as the pillar of light and the golden egg. At times, Mother Earth is referred to as the womb and Father Sky and Space as the *linga,* a symbol of male sexuality. In Puranic sacrificial rituals, the fire is called a linga, and the yoni, or hearth, is a symbol of female sexuality. Both are common Saivite symbols. The most commonly known linga is the fire linga, which is referred to as *Jyotirlinga.* In Hindu mythology, Jyotirlinga is one of the forms of the god Shiva.

In one myth, Shiva, as Jyotirlinga, asserts his supremacy over two other high gods, Brahma and Vishnu. The myth is told thusly:

> *One day, Brahma noticed Vishnu, with his thousand omniscient eyes, lying on the formless waters, supported by the thousand-headed serpent of the Infinite. Impressed by Vishnu's radiance, Brahma asked the eternal being who he was. Vishnu raised his sleepy lotus eyes, smiled, and beckoned to Brahma in a condescending manner. Brahma was offended by Vishnu's informal attitude, and responded, "How can you treat me as a master would his pupil? I am the cause of creation and destruction, the creator of a thousand universes, the source of all that exists!" Vishnu replied, "Don't you know that I am Narayana, creator, preserver, and destroyer of the worlds, eternal male, immortal source of the universe, and its center as well? Even thou are born of my indestructible body."*

Brahma and Vishnu thus argued bitterly above the formless sea, when a glorious, shimmering linga appeared before their eyes. The linga was a flamboyant pillar with the brilliance of a hundred fires, capable of consuming the universe. It was without

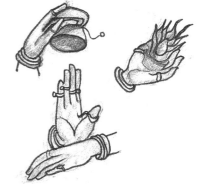

■ *These three drawings depict three hand gestures of Shiva. In his upper right hand, he carries the drum, whose sound symbolizes the creation of the cosmos. In his upper left hand, he carries the flame, which symbolizes the simultaneous destruction of the cosmos. Shiva's lower hands are together in a gesture of blessing and reassurance.*

beginning, without middle, and without end, incomparable and indescribable. Then the divine Vishnu, troubled as Brahma was by the flames, said to him, "We must look for the source of this fire. I shall go down in the form of a boar. You shall rise up in your manifestation of a swan."

Taking the shape of a blue boar with sharp tusks, a long snout and, firm, short feet, Vishnu plunged into the depths for a thousand years. However, despite his enduring effort, he could not find the base of the fire linga. Meanwhile, the white swan, with burning eyes and great wings, whose flight was as swift as the wind, soared for a thousand years to find the top of the pillar. He, too, was unable to reach it. Brahma was returning when he met the great Vishnu, likewise returning, weary and disconcerted. Suddenly they saw Shiva standing before them as Jyotirlinga. They bowed before him. Vishnu said to Shiva, "Our dispute has been blessed by you, the god of gods, since you appeared before us to put an end to our argument." Shiva replied, "I am supreme lord, undivided. I am three: Brahma, Vishnu and Shiva. I create, I maintain, I destroy."

Stories such as this one show Shiva's supremacy over all the other gods. Hindus have looked up to such sacred stories for examples of godlike behavior. They also gain insight into who and what it is they worship.

Sons of Shiva and Parvati

As Hindu mythology relates, Shiva and Parvati reside in the Himalaya Mountains with their sons, Ganesha and Skanda (who sometimes is called Kartikeya). Ganesha is an elephant-headed god, the remover of obstacles, who is invoked at the beginning of every Hindu undertaking. Skanda is an immortal warrior, the defender of the gods, who is associated with Agni and Indra.

Many different myths exist concerning the origin of Ganesha's elephant head. According to one account, Parvati, before starting to bathe one day, scraped the ointment from her body and mixed it with oils and other ointments. From this she formed a man's figure and gave it life by sprinkling it with water from the Ganges River. She then set this figure, her son Ganesha, outside the bathhouse door to stand guard. When Shiva tried to enter, Ganesha

■ This drawing depicts Shiva as the greatest of the three major Hindu gods. He appears as the Linga of Fire and is worshiped by the other two great gods, Brahma and Vishnu.

refused to let him in. As Shiva did not know him, he became angry and cut off Ganesha's head. When Parvati emerged and found her son dead, she was overwrought with grief. Shiva felt sympathy for his wife, so he sent a messenger to seek another head for the child. The first creature the messenger found was an elephant. He brought the elephant's head back and this was planted on Ganesha's shoulders.

Other versions of Ganesha's origin suggest that Shiva created him in response to a request by the gods and sages, who had realized that there was no overseer of good or bad deeds. Shiva pondered over this lack of a guide for some time, then turned toward Parvati. As he looked at her, a radiant youth of great beauty, endowed with the qualities of Shiva, sprang forth from his gaze. All the heavenly hosts were amazed and captivated by his beauty.

Parvati was jealous and angered by her husband's production of such a beautiful son. She cursed the son, wishing that he would become ugly and have an elephant's head. Shiva countered her curse by declaring that despite his son's elephantine head, he would be the guardian of successes and failures and would rule over all occasions. He declared that Ganesha would be great among gods, that he would be the god of wisdom and prudence, that he would be a scribe and learned in all the scriptures. Today, Ganesha is represented as a short, pot-bellied man with four arms and an elephant head.

The stories of Ganesha that have been handed down over the many centuries show the complexity of his personality. These stories point to the variety of traditions that have gone to create the complex portraits we have of Ganesha. They also show how Hinduism has been a fluid religion, even in its portraits of the ever-surviving characters that descend from Shiva.

One story of Ganesha and his brother, Kartikeya, tells how they were rivals for the same wives. To settle their dispute, they agreed that whoever first circled the world would win the wife of his choosing. Kartikeya set off and after a long, wearying excursion, he returned home. There he found Ganesha—who had never left—already married to both young women. The elephant-headed brother explained to Kartikeya that instead of making the painstaking journey around the world, he had simply circled around their father, Shiva, who is the equivalent of the universe!

In some myths, Kartikeya is married to Kumari. In many others, he is portrayed as someone not interested in women. He rides a peacock, carries bows and arrows, and has six heads and six pairs of arms. Accounts of Kartikeya's origin and his strange appearance vary. In one very popular myth, the demon Taraka was creating havoc in the heavens, and the gods discussed how they could put an end to this tyranny. They decided that they had to persuade Shiva to have a son who would kill Taraka.

Unfortunately, Shiva was engaged most deeply in meditation. At the same time, Parvati was also deeply absorbed in meditation. Shiva took no notice of her, nor she of him. Seeing this, the gods ordered Kama, the god of love, to approach Shiva, the great ascetic, and stir up a strong desire in his heart for Parvati. Kama obediently went to Mount Kailasha in the Himalaya Mountains, saw Shiva meditating, and found beautiful Parvati gathering flowers. Kama thought Shiva could be attracted by Parvati's beauty, so he drew his arrow and let it fly. As the arrow struck Shiva, desire awoke in his heart. But then Shiva not only saw Parvati—he also saw Kama. He realized that the god of love was trying to manipulate him. This made Shiva so angry that he burned Kama to ashes instantly.

Though desire had been aroused in his heart, Shiva, the lord of asceticism, did not give way to his passion. He consented to marry Parvati, but no children were born. Again, the gods decided to take matters into their own hands. They sent Agni as their ambassador to urge Shiva to beget a son. Agni, disguised as a bird, flew around, watching Shiva constantly. Finally, he managed to pick up a seed of the great god in his beak. As he flew, his burden seemed to grow heavier and heavier until finally, as he was passing over the river Ganges, he was forced to drop it. There, on the banks of the Ganges, arose a child as beautiful as the moon and as brilliant as the sun. This was Kartikeya. As he appeared on the bank of the Ganges, six royal women came to bathe. Each of them wanted this beautiful son as her own and wished to feed him. So the newborn god acquired six mouths, and was suckled by all of his foster mothers.

Vishnu and the Ten Avatars

In the period of the *Vedas*, Vishnu was a minor divinity. He was associated with the Aryan warrior-god, Indra. Gradually, Vishnu gained importance, and by the time of the great epics he was a paramount deva of the Hindu trinity: Brahma, Shiva, and Vishnu.

Vishnu is known as a powerful but kind god. He is a father-like figure and a just ruler. He is worshiped with great devotion, and little fear. The Vaishnavites (the followers of Vishnu) worship Vishnu as the greatest of the gods, the preserver, and the ever-present spirit.

Vishnu is most commonly depicted as a handsome young man dressed in royal robes, reclining with his wife, Lakshami, on the coil of the serpent Ananta (or Shesha). He has four hands with which he holds a conch shell, a discus, a club, and a lotus flower. The *Garuda*, a creature half man and half eagle, is Vishnu's *Vahana* (vehicle). Vishnu resides in a heavenly city called Vaikuntha, which is said to be made entirely of gold and precious jewels. This city is located on the mythical Mount Meru. The river Ganges, which according to some myths has its source in Vishnu's foot, flows through the city. In the pools of this heaven grow blue, red, and white lotuses. Vishnu and Lakshami sit amid the white lotuses, where they both radiate like the sun.

Vishnu's role as preserver seems to have developed as a means to maintain balance in the universe between good and evil powers. In the normal course of events, the gods and demons are evenly matched in the world. At times, however, demons seem to gain the upper hand. During such times, Vishnu, as preserver, intervenes to restore balance by descending to earth in the form of an incarnation. "Whenever the Sacred Law fails, and evil raises its head, I (Vishnu) take embodied birth. To guard the righteous, to root out sinners, and to establish the Sacred Law, I am born from age to age." (*Bhagavad Gita* IV.6-8)

Hindu mythology holds that there are ten incarnations of Vishnu, called avatars. During each incarnation, Vishnu has a specific task to perform. Of the ten avatars, four are animals. In the form of *matsya* (a fish), Vishnu saved the sage Manu and the sacred Vedas from a great flood. Also in this flood, the gods lost

■ *The beneficent god Vishnu reclines on the thousand-headed primordial serpent. From his navel emerges Brahma, the world creator. The world created by Brama is ruled by Vishnu for a* **yuga** *(a long period of time), after which it is dissolved and recreated. Thus the cycle of* **samsara** *goes on.*

for a time the elixir of their immortality. Vishnu assumed the form of *kurma*, a great tortoise, and dove to the bottom of the ocean to retrieve the potent drink.

When the demon Hiranyaksha cast the earth to the bottom of the sea, Vishnu became *varaha*, the boar. He plunged into the depths, saved the earth and spread it on top of the waters to float. Another demon, the tyrant Hiranyakashapa, had obtained a special privilege through which he could be killed neither by human nor animal, neither inside nor outside of his home, nor by day nor by night. He lived without fear and wreaked great havoc wherever he went. To overcome the demon, Vishnu took the form of the *narasimha* (half human and half lion) and killed Hiranyakashapa on the threshold of his home at sunset.

Other avatars were human in form. A popular legend told of the three great strides with which Vishnu stepped over the universe and foiled the demon-king, Bali. The demon-king had control of the earth, so Vishnu devised a plan to deceive the king. Vishnu took the form of Vamana, the dwarf, and asked the king if he could have as much space as he could cover in three steps. Believing that the dwarf could only cover a small space, Bali agreed. Then Vishnu became Vamana, a great giant, and strode across the earth and the heavens. At another time, the *kshattriyas* (the warrior class) threatened to oust the Brahmins from power. So Vishnu was born as the Brahmin Parashurama, known as Rama with the Axe, to assert the sanctity of the caste system.

Traditionally, the ninth avatar of Vishnu was the religious sage, the Buddha. Some Hindu texts state that Vishnu, as the Buddha, taught wrong religious ideas to evil people. Other texts claim that the Buddha was born to save innocent animals, as part of his doctrine of nonviolence to all living things.

The tenth avatar is the only incarnation of Vishnu that is yet to come. It is believed that this manifestation of the great god, referred to as *Kalki*, will appear at the "end" of the present time, riding a white horse and holding a flaming sword.

All ten avatars were recognized in the sacred scriptures by around the eleventh century C.E. By far, however, the most widely worshiped of these gods were Rama and Krishna, the seventh and eighth avatars of Vishnu.

■ *This drawing depicts the emblems that are always carried by Vishnu: a discus, a club, a lotus, and a conch shell.*

The Adventures of Rama, Prince of Ayodhya

Rama, the prince of Ayodha, was the seventh avatar of Vishnu. The great epic poem, the *Ramayana* ("adventures of Rama") tells of Rama's life. As we have said, Rama's task in this incarnation was to subdue the powerful ten-headed Ravana, demonking of Sri Lanka. The demon-king's demise is the central theme of the *Ramayana*.

The king Ravana was said to be a devoted student of Vedic rituals. Brahma rewarded his devotion with a gift of invulnerability. Ravana could be killed neither by god nor demon. However, Ravana misused the gift of Brahma; he conquered the heavens and brought all the gods to Sri Lanka where they served him in chains. Indra became his wreath-maker, Brahma his messenger, Agni his cook, Vishnu his steward, Shiva his barber, Vayu his sweeper, and Varuna his water-carrier. Thus Ravana's uncompromising devotion to the god Brahma was so profound that it shook the foundations of the celestial, atmospheric, and earthly worlds.

The gods appealed to Vishnu for a solution to their predicament. Vishnu declared that Ravana had been too proud to ask for immunity from mere mortals. As a result, he would be slain because of a woman, by a human, and aided by animals. Then Vishnu incarnated himself as Rama, a mere mortal. However, he was the oldest son of the king Dasratha. Through the story of Rama's life, we are led to the king's demise.

Rama married a princess named Sita. Shortly after the marriage, Dasratha decided to retire and make his son Rama king. Dasratha's queen, however, asked the king for a favor he had promised to her long before. She asked that her son Bharata take the throne as king, and that Rama be exiled for fourteen years. Dasratha was utterly disheartened, but he kept his word.

Rama wanted to go into exile alone, but his wife Sita and his brother and best friend, Lakshamana, insisted on accompanying him. So, with all the loyal subjects lamenting their departure, the three companions set off into the forest. Rama's father, Dasratha, died of grief within a few days.

In the meantime, Bharata was returning from a journey for what he thought was to be the coronation of his brother, Rama. When he learned what had happened, he was appalled. Bharata went to the forest to persuade his elder brother to return to the throne. However, Rama politely refused, saying that he could not oppose his father's word. Bharata returned to the kingdom but reigned only as a viceroy, preserving a pair of Rama's sandals on the throne as a symbol of the rightful king.

The demon-king Ravana's sister, Surpanakha, often visited the forest where Rama, Sita, and Lakshamana lived. She fell in love with Rama, but he resisted her advances because he loved Sita. Angered, Surpanakha turned her affections toward Lakshamana. Lakshamana ignored her completely. When she persisted, he became very annoyed and cut off her nose and ears.

Surpanakha was crazed. She decided to entice her brother, Ravana, with details of Sita's beauty. She told him what a perfect wife Sita would be for him. Ravana was intrigued, but he was also well aware of Rama's power. Ravana knew that it would be most difficult to take Sita from Rama.

To get Sita, Ravana sent an enchanted deer to the forest. This deer was so beautiful that Sita asked Rama and Lakshamana to catch it for her. While the two brothers chased the deer, Ravana disguised himself as an ascetic. He approached Sita and took her away in his chariot to his golden palace in Sri Lanka. On the way, Jatayu, Rama's bird friend, saw them. He tried to save Sita but was mortally wounded.

Meanwhile, the two brothers returned from their quest to capture the enchanted deer. They found Jatayu, and learned from the wounded bird what had happened. Greatly disturbed, Rama made plans to rescue Sita. He made an alliance with the monkey-king Sugriva, who presented Rama with an army of monkeys and bears. The general of this army was the mighty Hanuman, son of Vayu, the wind god. Before anyone else could reach Sri Lanka, Hanuman had flown to Ravana's palace and found Sita alone in a garden. He gave her Rama's ring as a token, and assured her that Rama would rescue her. However, Hanuman was caught by Ravana's guards, who brought him before the demon-king. Ravana ordered the guards to wrap oily rags around Hanuman's tail and to set fire to them. But Hanuman managed to escape, jumping from building to building with his burning tail trailing behind him. He set fire to all the buildings of the golden palace.

Because he was able to fly, Hanuman flew back to the mainland where he rejoined Rama. Upon hearing Hanuman's story, Rama went to Sri Lanka with the monkey army and a mighty battle was fought before the gates of the city. During the battle Hanuman, with golden yellow skin, red face and enormous tail, was terrifyingly valiant. But his greatest service was his flight to the Himalayas from which he brought herbs to cure Rama and Lakshamana when they were wounded.

The forces of Ravana fought vigorously, but all the demons, including Ravana's two brothers, were killed. Finally, Rama and Ravana faced each other in combat. The earth trembled as they fought, and the whole company of gods watched. At one point, Rama felt that Ravana had begun to overpower him. Rama drew out the dreaded brahmastra, a magic weapon fused with the

A huge Hanuman (the monkey god) relief on the banks of the Nasik River overlooks washermen. Hanuman is the symbol of an ideal devotee and of renunciation.

energy of many gods. He strung the weapon on his bow and, whispering a Vedic mantra, shot it toward Ravana and killed him. At that moment, all the gods showered Rama with wreaths. Rama and Sita were reunited and returned to their kingdom with Lakshamana and Hanuman.

It is said that during Rama's reign, the world knew unprecedented peace. However, the people of his kingdom began to gossip about Sita. They charged that because she lived in Ravana's palace she might not be fit to be the queen. The people mistrusted Sita so Rama felt obliged to send his queen into exile, even though she was pregnant at the time. She took refuge in a forest hermitage where she gave birth to twin sons, Luv and Kush.

When the twins were fifteen years old, they went to visit the capital and were recognized by their father. Rama then sent for Sita. He called together a great assembly so that Sita could publicly declare her innocence. In front of the assembly, Sita called upon Earth, her mother (for Sita had been born in a furrow), to prove her innocence. The earth opened and swallowed her into its womb. Rama was heartbroken and wished to follow her. He walked into the river, where Brahma's voice welcomed him into heaven.

For Hindus, the characters of the *Ramayana* are models of human existence. Rama was not only a just king, but an ideal son for having honored his father's promise. Sita was an ideal wife because she gave up queenly comforts to be with her husband. Lakshamana was a model brother who, like Sita, left the comforts of royalty to support Rama. Hanuman was the ideal devotee who followed and served faithfully. All of these characters are celebrated in Hindu households and frequently mentioned in Hindu sacred and secular literature.

Krishna

One of Hinduism's most widely worshiped gods is Krishna, the eighth avatar of Vishnu. His popularity may be due in part to his extremely colorful character. From his childhood, Krishna performed many great feats. As a youth, he dallied with milkmaids. As a young man he performed the task for which he was incarnated. And in middle age, as a great ruler, he took part in the mythological Mahabharata War, which is described in the great epic *Mahabharata*.

The story of Krishna starts with the demon Kansa, a tyrant who usurped the throne of his own father, Ugrasena, and imprisoned him. Kansa had heard from a sage that a son of one of his female kin would bring about his demise. So, the demon-king ordered all her children to be slain. Immediately, six children were put to death. However, her seventh child, Balarama, and her eighth child, Krishna, were miraculously saved and secretly given to foster parents. When Kansa learned of their escapes, he ordered a massacre. Again the brothers were saved. Nanda and Yasoda, Krishna's foster parents, fled to Gokula and reared the boys among the milkmaids and cowherds.

In early childhood, Krishna revealed a dual character. Sometimes, he was a normal, lovable baby. At other times, he exhibited extraordinary superhuman strength. One popular myth tells of Krishna's encounter with the demon Putna, an ogress who, disguised as a beautiful girl, would suckle babies with her poisoned breasts. But her poison could not harm Krishna—he sucked so hard that he drew all the life out of Putna. The youthful Krishna often amused himself by playing pranks on his adoptive mother and the milkmaids of Gokula. He stole curds and butter, raided orchards for fruit, upset pails of milk, and blamed the other children for all his mischief.

As a young man, Krishna is renowned for amorous adventures with numerous maidens. One tale tells of his encounter with a hunch-backed, ugly maiden, Kubja, who was bearing perfumed oils for tyrant-demon Kansa. When Krishna asked her for some of the perfume, she rubbed it on his body. In return, Krishna pressed on her feet with his own foot, lifted her chin and straightened her. Other adventures with a milkmaid named Radha are told in stories noted for their beauty and sensuous descriptions. These stories also have a spiritual meaning because in them, Krishna symbolizes the universal soul, and the milkmaids are individual souls longing to be united with the Ultimate Reality and achieve enlightenment.

All through Krishna's growing years, Kansa continued to plot his death, but Krishna was always able to fend off the tyrant's

■ *The love of cowherd Krishna and his beloved Radha is celebrated in hundreds of Hindu songs and stories. Their love symbolizes the longing of devotees for their personal deities.*

attempts. Krishna destroyed the snake demon Kaliya by dancing on his head. He also swallowed a fire demon sent to consume the young god and his companions.

Finally, the demon-king Kansa master-minded a plot to slay both Krishna and his brother Balarama. To kill them, he would host a series of athletic games and invite them both. On their way to the court of Mathura where the games would be held, Krishna and Balarama encountered many of Kansa's cohorts—demons and monsters and ogres. Krishna and Balarama thwarted these evil beings, just as they did to the host of gruesome demons that appeard at the games. Finally, Kansa himself opposed Krishna, only to have the prophecy of the sage come true: Krishna slayed Kansa. Having done so, Krishna restored Ugrasena, the rightful king, to the throne. He also traveled to the underworld to bring back to life the six brothers who were killed by Kansa at birth.

Then Krishna abandoned the pastoral life and became a feudal prince, thus entering the last phase of his life.

Krishna's struggles with the forces of evil climaxed in the Mahabharata War between his kinsmen, the Pandavas and the Kauravas. In a prewar council, Krishna tried to reconcile the opposing parties, but to no avail. Then, since he had promised not to participate actively in the skirmish, Krishna disguised himself as the charioteer of Arjuna, a member of the Pandava family. Arjuna asked his charioteer to draw up to a point from which they could survey the battlefield. While looking down on the opposed forces of his family, Arjuna questioned the reasoning of kinsmen killing kinsmen.

Krishna's response to Arjuna—contained in the well-known Hindu scripture, the *Bhagavad Gita*—regards religious obligation and devotion to God. In his discussion, Krishna informs Arjuna of the higher universal order to which he must be true—that which is beyond the temporary existence of this world. He points out that Arjuna is of the warrior caste, and that he must fulfill his duty as a warrior. Krishna also tells Arjuna that though his body may die, his soul is indestructible.

Stories of Krishna appear in many Hindu texts, but the most well-known and respected of these are the teachings found in the *Bhagavad Gita*. The *Bhagavad Gita* is a very short section (about eighteen chapters) of the 100,000 verses of the *Mahabharata*. Teachings in the *Bhagavad Gita* are revered by Hindus of many sects. Many Hindus have memorized verses from the *Gita*, and often parts of the *Gita* are spoken during daily devotions. The teachings of the *Gita* are spoken by Krishna in this scripture whose author is unknown.

Instead of bringing out differences among the various systems of Hindu thought and practice, the *Bhagavad Gita* emphasizes the points of agreement among them. It thereby brings about a religious and philosophical unity. It discusses *sva-dharma*, the individual's duties or social obligations. It stresses the significance of all the castes. Furthermore, this text recommends total devotion, or *bhakti*, as the most effective form of religion. It assumes that there is a personal god who blesses with divine grace the devoted worshipers.

In the *Bhagavad Gita*, Krishna describes his relation to his devotees:

A leaf, a flower, a fruit, or water
whoever offers to me with devotion—
that same, proffered in devotion by
one whose soul is pure, I accept.

Even if a person of extremely vile conduct
worships me being devoted to none else,
he is to be reckoned as righteous, for he
has engaged himself in action in the right
spirit. Quickly does he become of righteous
soul and obtains eternal peace. Know for
certain that my devotee perishes not.

For those who take refuge in me,
even though they be lowly born, women,
vaisyas, (the third Hindu caste)and
also sudras (the lowest Hindu caste)
even they attain to the highest goal.

Arjuna's relationship with Krishna existed on many levels. He was Krisha's warrior and student, and he was completely devoted to him. Arjuna's devotion to Krisha was intensified when Krishna revealed to him his awesome forms—as all gods, Brahman, the soul of the world. Thus Arjuna's chief feelings for Krishna were awe inspired:

You (Krishna) are the father of the universe,
of all that moves and all that moves not,
itsworshipful and worthy teacher.
You have no equal—what in the three worlds
could equal you O power beyond compare?

So, reverently prostrating my body,
I crave your grace, O blessed lord
As father to son, as friend to friend,
as lover to beloved, bear with me, god.

The relationship Arjuna had with Krishna is an example of an individual having a personal god. This kind of relationship is further elaborated by poet-sages throughout India from the eighth to the sixteenth century. These writers have produced widely popular literature.

Krishna and Balarama spent the last days of their lives in a forest refuge where Balarama died in his sleep. Krishna mourned alone under a fig tree on the bank of a river but a passing hunter mistook him for a deer and wounded him fatally.

The Supreme Goddess Mahadevi Shakti

Goddesses have been revered since the pre-Aryan time of the Indus Valley culture, when devotees attributed the fertility of the land to a maternal deity. By the Vedic period, significant female deities had emerged. These include Prithvi, the goddess earth, Vac, the goddess of speech and wisdom.

In the epics, the consorts—Sarasvati, Parvati and Lakshami—of the three major gods had become quite prominent in themselves. Sarasvati (associated with Vac) is regarded as the goddess of all the creative arts, sciences and knowledge. Parvati, the wife of Shiva, is associated with the Himalaya Mountains. Like her husband, she has immense ascetic and erotic characteristics. Lakshami, Vishnu's consort, is associated with the lotus, symbol of power and good luck.

Though these goddesses came to hold much respect in the minds of goddess devotees, the great goddess Mahadevi Shakti is the one ultimate reality. In addition to the three major goddesses, numerous minor goddesses are revered by Hindus. However, all the goddesses are manifestations of Mahadevi, the great goddess. With the popularity of the sixth-century *Markandya Purana*, worship of the great goddess had become well established. At present, goddess worship is visible primarily in the villages, and many of these goddesses have only local reputations. In the minds of villagers, all these local goddesses are associated with the great goddess, Mahadevi Shakti.

Mahadevi is an active and powerful female, who is attentive to the stability of the world and to the needs of her devotees. She is worshiped for her different aspects, including those of the great maternal goddess and the devoted consort or wife. Her character has a beneficent side as well as a destructive side. Hindus perceive the two sides of Mahadevi as a natural part of an orderly universe containing both positive and negative forces—life and death, creation and destruction, vigor and rest.

The complexity of Mahadevi Shakti—in such forms as Sati, Parvati, Durga, and Kali—is expressed in a variety of roles which she shares with her husband, Shiva. She is both mild and fierce. In her mild form she is Sati, daughter of a sage who marries Shiva against her father's wishes. Later she sacrifices herself on her father's sacrificial fire because he does not approve of Shiva, her husband. After some time, Sati is reborn as Parvati, the daughter of Himavat, god of mountains. She practices austere yoga, Shiva is impressed by her yogic powers and marries her again.

In her fierce form, the great goddess is Durga. Durga was created out of angry flames that issued forth from the mouths of Brahma, Vishnu, Shiva, and other gods. She was specifically

■ *The Great Goddess Shakti, or Devi. Like Shiva, Shakti is both auspicious as well as terrifying. Here she is shown in her auspicious form, surrounded by major Hindu gods: Brahma, Vishnu, Shiva, and Surya (the Sun God).*

created by the gods to kill the buffalo demon, Mahisha, who, by abstinence, had gained the strength to drive the gods from their celestial kingdom.

Durga was born fully grown and beautiful, riding a tiger from the Himalayan forests. She was immediately armed by the gods, and in each of her ten hands she held special weapons: Vishnu's discus, Shiva's trident (three-pronged spear), Agni's flaming dart, Indra's thunderbolt, and Varuna's conch shell, among others. With these weapons, Durga killed the buffalo-demon and returned the gods to their rightful kingdom.

On another occasion, the gods appealed to the goddess Durga to eliminate the demon brothers, Sumbha and Nisumbha. Shiva had blessed the brothers with immortality because they had performed austerities that made the gods tremble. As a goddess capable of defeating demons, Durga agreed to combat the brothers. When she appeared before Sumbha, his passion was aroused and he desired to possess her. She agreed to consent only if he could overcome her in battle. Sumbha accepted the condition hotly, not realizing that the immortality granted him was protection from gods only, and not from goddesses. And so Durga defeated the demon and his brother with ease.

Despite her grace, Durga combatted many demons who had obtained boons protecting them from gods and men. Her primary role was to maintain and protect cosmic order by appearing periodically to battle such demon oppressors.

Kali, "the black one," personifies the most terrifying aspects of Mahadevi Shakti. She leaves bloodshed, disease, and death in her wake. Her body is decked with terrible ornaments made from bones; a string of human skulls adorns her neck. She wields a sword in one hand, a dagger in another, and the severed heads of two giants hang, dripping blood, from her two other hands. Her hair is wildly disheveled, tusks protrude from her face, a third eye peers out from the middle of her forehead, and she is often portrayed with her tongue hanging out. Having overcome the power of death, she dwells in the cremation ground, seating herself on corpses.

One myth tells of how Kali rid the world of the dreaded tyrant Raktabija. Wherever a drop of his blood fell, thousands of demons would appear. Thus Kali slew him and drained all the blood from his body.

With all her gruesome characteristics, Kali became an ultimate representative of death. Many Hindus believe that spiritual enlightenment can be achieved if the terrifying aspects of this deity, the image of all life's fear and pain, can be overcome.

Through centuries of change, an often expanding pantheon of Hindu goddesses and gods encompassed a broad range of disparate beliefs. Common among the philosophies and sects that emerged was a goal to perceive the ultimate reality on a more personal level than had previously been thought possible. This desire grew in popularity and blossomed into an influential movement based on personal devotion to an individual deity.

Bhakti, or Devotionalism

The most important theme throughout the epics and the *Puranas* was that of bhakti, or devotion. Early bhakti reflected the cultural and social changes that were taking place in Hindu society before and during Islamic rule. The Bhakti movement expressed a great change from traditionally Vedic-based ceremonies and attitudes, although the authority of the *Vedas* was never renounced. More recent religious texts stress the independence of Bhakti religion from other means of salvation.

Bhakti was conceived as a way of life, a selfless and complete surrender to God. Members of the movement invoked their goddess or god by name and recited hymns of praise, always being mindful of the deity. Devotees were to acknowledge no difference between themselves and others. They were required to be free of jealousy, falsehood, envy, and injury. Nor were Bhakti devotees encouraged to take pride in their birthright or wealth. The teachings of Bhakti implied that a person's birth and caste had no significant influence on their salvation—salvation depended only on a devotee's purity of heart.

Devotional emphasis also carried over into social attitudes. Material poverty was looked on with favor. Great compassion was shown for the persecuted, distressed, and despised. And caste distinctions were declared irrelevant. Women have played significant roles in the Hindu tradition as mothers and wives;

however throughout Indian history, whenever women were able to break away from social and religious customs, they have magnificently contributed to various other fields of life. In the area of religion, two women who come to mind are the saint-poetesses of the Bhakti movement: Lalleshwari (fourteenth century) and Mira Bhai (sixteenth century).

The writers of the Bhakti movement (eighth to seventeenth centuries) chose to write in languages spoken by the common people of local regions. This was because Sanskrit, the language of the *Puranas*, was only taught to the learned of the Brahmin caste. Sanskrit was the language of the elite, even though in earlier times it contained some popular expressions that may have come from some less-educated people. The Bhakti writers chose not to write in Sanskrit to make their literature most accessible.

The language of devotion was the language of human emotion, at times so intense that it was painful, highly moving, and intensely personal. The poet-sages related their relationship with God in terms of love, friendship, despair, and joy. They implied that the goal of bhakti was salvation in very personal terms, not merely an ambiguous union with the impersonal Brahman (Universal Soul). Salvation through bhakti included an eternal relationship of blissful devotion. In this relationship, unlike that pictured by the earlier ascetics, the devotee and the Ultimate Reality would remain separate. In the words of one poet, devotion was "to taste sugar, not become sugar."

Intense devotional fervor was evident in the poetry of the movement. The poets produced thousands of poems in various regional languages. The poets belonged to the people, and integrated them by conveying this religious movement from region to region. Though they themselves were from different social levels of Hindu society, the poets helped keep Brahmanism alive. They constantly revitalized Hindu ideas and beliefs, making this religion available to all people.

Because of this facilitating role, poets who possessed outstanding powers of expression became quite popular all over India. An eighth-century poet from the south of India wrote:

I am false, my heart is false, my love is false,
But I, this sinner, can win thee if I weep before thee, O lord,

Thou who art sweet like
honey, nectar, and the juice of sugar cane!
Please bless me so that I can reach thee.

Lalleswari, the fourteenth-century Kashmiri devotional poetess wrote in opposition to temple worship:

Image is of stone, temple is of stone, Above and Below are
one, which of them will you worship, O foolish Pandit?
Because within you lies the union of mind and soul.

She mocked religious persecution and discrimination, saying:

Shiva permeates this Universe
Do not discriminate between a Hindu and a Muslim
If thou art sharp enough, know thyself.

Some have abandoned home
some the forest abode
What use the hermitage if thou controllest not thine mind.

Basavanna, a twelfth-century devotional poet from South India, offered his body to his personal god because he, unlike rich devotees, could not afford to build a temple:

The rich
will make temples for Shiva
What shall I,
a poor man do?

My legs are pillars,
the body the shrine,
the head a cupola of gold.

Listen, O Lord,
things standing shall fall,
but the moving ever shall stay.

In this poem, the poet's body is compared with a temple. He reminds us that the temple has become a meaningless monument with its original symbolism forgotten. By identifying his body with a temple, the poet makes his body sacred and he offers himself to God. He emphasizes that rich people only make temples, but poor people themselves become temples, exhibiting the intensity and purity of their devotion.

Poet-sages were considered godlike humans who not only continued Hindu traditions throughout Muslim rule but spread it throughout India, integrating local traditions into a national religion. They were considered a link between the human and the divine and were symbols of the Hindu idea that an element of the sacred dwells within each individual.

It was because of devotional saints that all the Hindu religious sects were woven together in a complex system. However, political integration did not follow social and cultural integration. In 712 c.e., a twenty-year-old Arab military leader named Muhammad ibn Kasim swept into the Indus Valley, introducing the challenge of Islam and eras of change that would alter the face of Hinduism forever.

CHAPTER 5

Political and
Social Change

*T*he eighth century C.E. brought the beginning of an endless series of changes and challenges to India and to Hinduism. With new religions, new rulers, new laws, and new saints, Hinduism proved to be a stable and flexible religious way of life.

Islam in India

Islam came to India first as a religion, then as a political force. In the eighth century, Arabs infiltrated the Indian continent. Almost three centuries later the Afghans, the Turks and the Persians, all Muslims, came to conquer but stayed as the rulers. By the thirteenth century Muslim rule had blossomed throughout most of northern India. The cultural and the political center of the new rulers was in Delhi.

The Islamic culture in India reached its apex of brilliance under the Mughal empire. The Mughal dynasty was founded by a Persian warrior chief Babur in the early sixteenth century. The empire reached its splendour during the reign of his great grandson Akbar the Great (ruled 116-1605 C.E.). The empire eventually declined by the beginning of the eighteenth century.

Muslim rulers dominated the political and cultural landscape of India for almost nine centuries. Initially, Hindus responded to Muslim rule and the expansion of Islam in a variety of ways. Many Hindus converted to Islam, but the majority remained loyal to their religious heritage. For those who chose non-Muslim religions, Muslim rulers imposed a special tax. In addition, Hindu temples were demolished, and countless idols were destroyed. The Muslims considered the Hindus to be pagan pantheon worshipers, and they especially despised the Hindu tradition of image worship. As a result, a considerable and enduring hostility arose in the gulf, with misunderstanding and suspicion running rampant between Indians who were Hindu and Indians who were Muslim.

Significant interaction between Hindus and Muslims occurred only at more sophisticated levels of each religion and in the teachings of certain poet-sages. In addition, Muslim rulers supported scholars and artists—among whom Hindus numbered significantly. As a result, Hinduism was influenced by Islam, and Islam was likewise influenced by Hinduism. In particular, Islam stifled much of the elitism of Brahmanic traditions, allowing devotional movements such as Bhakti to progress. Islamic mysticism (or *Sufism* as it is popularly known) had much in common with the Hindu Bhakti movement. Both emphasized a direct personal relationship with God, and together they produced a religious outlook whose outstanding aspect was complete independence from organized sects and orthodox scriptures.

The movement toward devotional worship was the focus of Kabir, one of the most popular poet-sages of the era. Though Kabir had been raised as a Muslim and influenced by Sufism, he taught a simple form of Hinduism. His teachings emphasized love of God and the idea that God would return that love despite caste and creed. Though Kabir worshiped Rama, he taught that no matter what the divine entity of any religion was called, be it Rama or Allah (the one god of the Muslims), it was the same God. In his writings, Kabir conveyed the simple nature of devotional worship:

> *I do not ring the temple bell,*
> *I do not set the idol on its throne,*

I do not worship the image with flowers
It is not the austerities that mortify the flesh
which are pleasing to the lord,
When you leave off your clothes and kill your senses,
you do not please the lord.
The man who is kind and who practices righteousness,
who remains passive amidst the affairs of the world,
who considers all creatures on earth as his own self,
He attains the Immortal Being, the true God is ever with him.

By the time the Mughal emperor Akbar came to power in the fifteenth century, an active sea route had been established from Europe to India, with many foreign merchants planting themselves along the Indian coastline.

Soon after, in the 1540's, a Christian mission was introduced by Saint Francis Xavier. Among his Jesuit followers were holy people who tried to convert Akbar. Though interested in Christian beliefs, Akbar was intrigued by other religions as well. Led by his curiosity, Akbar tried to introduce religious tolerance to his empire. As an example, he lifted the special tax on non-Muslims. This enraged Muslims to the degree that Akbar's successor, Aurangzeb, reimposed the tax and devastated many Hindu temples.

British Rule

By 1700 C.E., the Mughal Empire, which had flourished from the middle of the sixteenth century, was forced into decline by the Maratha tribes of central India. By this time as well, European traders and clergy had established tiny trading settlements and missionary centers along various coastal regions. British and French traders began to move vigorously into the political vacuum left by the Mughals. They financed many colonies in India to protect their interests there. Within fifty years, the British East India Company had gained control over India's most prosperous provinces. By 1818, the British were in control of the entire Indian subcontinent, including present-day India, Pakistan, Bangladesh, and Sri Lanka.

The British influence, though shorter in duration than the long Muslim rule, was much more disturbing to the Hindu

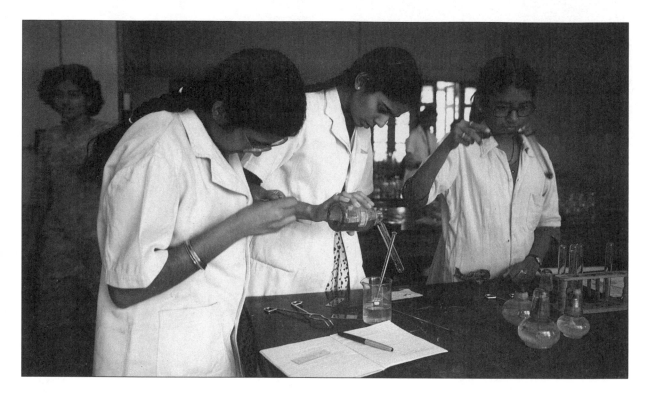

■ *Hindu women, like Hindu men, are being educated in arts and modern sciences at universities. Although the number of educated women is not as high as that of men, it is growing every year.*

outlook. The British government introduced nonreligious institutions, new economic institutions, and Western education to India. As a result, a growing portion of the population became literate, and occupations traditionally reserved for only one class of Hindus were suddenly open to all. Also, secular law and order diminished the authority of the Hindu religious moral code. British rule, then, disrupted and changed some of the basic ideas of Hinduism. It also altered the society in which Hindus had lived.

From major Indian cities like Calcutta, Bombay, and Madras, a worldwide exchange of goods began. People from all sections of society were engaged in trade. With work in the factories that were being built, millions of Hindus found jobs and freed themselves from social and religious obligations. A new merchant class developed, the members of which were free to adopt whatever form of religion they wished. Thus, economic independence helped to bring about religious choice.

The British found themselves ruling a population that spoke fourteen different major literary languages and hundreds of dialects. Therefore, the new rulers incorporated the English language into teaching in the schools and colleges. Public education offered by Hindu and Muslim religious institutions was minimal and a privilege for the select few. The British government introduced English schools that were open to everyone. In 1817, the Hindu College was established in Calcutta. And soon, Christian missionaries opened similar schools and colleges for both women and men in major Indian cities.

At the time of the Christian missionaries, some of the traditional Hindu beliefs and ancient doctrines had degenerated in destructive customs. These customs had survived into the era of British rule only because Hindus considered them to be socially and religiously normal. Christian missionaries from the West brought principles that challenged some of the customs.

One such custom was the caste system, which justified hereditary occupations and unequal distribution of opportunities. Hindus considered the caste system to be part of the normal course of life. The miserable conditions of the lower classes were also considered normal. Domination over and harsh treatment of women had become common. This can be seen in religiously condoned codes that forced young girls (mere children) into marriage and denied the right of remarriage to widows, even though they might be child brides. It can also be found in the practice of *sati,* which required a wife to burn herself on the funeral pyre of her husband. Finally, Christianity challenged the self-centered philosophy of Hinduism. Unlike Christians, Hindus taught that material desires were valueless and that happiness lay in personal liberation from the world and not in trying to transform it into a better place for everyone.

As a result of Western influence, many Indians turned a doubting eye on the traditions of Hinduism. Sophisticated Hindus became uncomfortable with their religion after comparing it to the ethical standards of the Western countries. At the same time, European scholars researched India's forgotten past. They uncovered records of a greater, pre-Islamic India in which brilliant systems of thought were developed and great works of literature and art were created. Hindu religious leaders called on the young people to identify with that ancient heritage.

By the end of the eighteenth century, a passionate nationalism with religious overtones began to grow in the minds of the educated. They recognized that the countries of the West were leaders in science and technology, but they believed that the East was the world's center of spiritual culture. During the nineteenth century, several important reforms were passed—partly on the initiative of liberal British administrators and partly as a result of pressure from English-educated Indians. A number of prominent Hindu figures emerged at this time to lead their religion into reform.

Rammohan Roy (1772-1833)

The first reformist, Rammohan Roy, was called the father of modern India. He radically changed many social and religious customs that had grown like cancers within a once healthy and vibrant religious tradition.

Rammohan Roy was born of devout Brahmin parents in Bengal, and early in his life, he showed an intense interest in religion. He traveled extensively and was fluent in several languages. Roy mastered the Upanishadic scriptures and considered them the core of Hinduism. He joined the British government and rose as high as a non-British person could in the Bengal Civil Service. Due to his successful administrative job, he was able to retire at the age of forty-two. After his retirement, Roy decided to settle permanently in Calcutta, which was then the political and intellectual capital of India.

For the next sixteen years, Rammohan Roy devoted himself to the work of enlightenment and reform. Earlier in his life, he had witnessed the death of his sister-in-law in the act of sati. She had been forced on to her husband's funeral pyre and held there with long poles while the sound of drums drowned out her screams. Horrified by this experience with such a Hindu tradition, Roy became a vehement opponent of sati. He founded, edited, and published several newspapers. Through print media published in several languages he campaigned against sati and other Hindu customs such as child marriage, image worship, and the worship of numerous gods. In 1829, Roy supported the government's decision to abolish by law the practice of sati. He then continued to fight for numerous other social reforms.

Later, having been inspired by some religious concepts he read in the Bible, such as Christian brotherhood and charity, Roy founded a religious society named *Brahmo Samaj* (Society of God). The members of this society—usually educated and of high social position—were called *brahmos*. Brahmos met weekly for congregational-style meetings that were quite unusual for Hinduism. The only rituals in their religious services were praying, the singing of hymns, and the giving of sermons based on Hindu scriptures.

Debendranath Tagore (1817-1905)

After Roy's death, the Brahmo Samaj society came under the leadership of Debendranath Tagore, the son of a financial supporter of the society. He had started a small association that met monthly to discuss religious questions. In 1843, he merged his group with the remnant of Roy's, preserving the original name, Brahmo Samaj, but injecting a new spirit into the organization. Like Rammohan Roy, Tagore's group opposed image worship. The members of the organization were young men who belonged to the upper Brahmin caste and they wore a sacred thread as the sign of their Brahmin birth.

Brahmos declared that the final authority in religion was to be found not in the ancient scriptures but in human reason and conscience. All its members were asked to give up their caste identities. They fought against child marriage and attacked the tradition of having more than one wife, causing an uproar among the upper Hindu classes. Although Brahmo Samaj is no longer a very strong religious society, its impact was tremendous during the second half of the nineteenth century. It substantially altered public opinion. Unfortunately, a sharp difference of opinion between Tagore and one of the society's most energetic members, Keshab Chandra Sen, divided the group and weakened it.

Sen founded discussion groups and schools, organized famine relief, advocated the remarriage of widows, and encouraged the education of women. He insisted that the members of Brahmo Samaj discontinue wearing the sacred thread used by high-caste

Hindus. Tagore, in spite of his open-mindedness, could not let go of the distinctive religious sign. So he withdrew from active leadership and continued the work Roy had begun, that of rediscovering and reviving Hindu monotheism (belief in one god).

Dayananda Sarasvati (1824-1883)

At the same time that the Brahmo Samaj society emerged, a very different movement was launched by a reformer named Dayananda Sarasvati. Sarasvati was born of wealthy Brahmin parents in the state of Saivite Gujarat. Following the death of his sister and his uncle, he contemplated the problems of life and afterlife. At at the age of twenty-one, Sarasvati became an ascetic and studied with a teacher who loathed the *Puranas* texts and all the popular gods of Hinduism. Sarasvati then traveled throughout India, acquiring many varied and influential experiences that caused him to question what he believed were perverted traditions of Hinduism.

In 1860, Sarasvati became the student of a blind guru, Swami Virajananda—great Vedic scholar. For four years , Sarasvati learned the scriptures in their purest form. He determined to oppose the corruptions of Hinduism with the truths he found in the Vedas. He began his own crusade by lecturing in Sanskrit, but in 1874, Sarasvati began to lecture in the simple Hindi of the common people. The following year, he founded the Arya Samaj (Noble Society).

Like Rommohan Roy, Sarasvati denounced Hindu polytheism (belief in many gods). He considered the *Vedas* the only authority from which the precepts of Hinduism could be drawn. He said that the existence of an untouchable caste, child marriage, subjugation of women by men, and the worship of images was not recommended in the *Vedas*. Furthermore, he claimed that Hindu castes had no place in true Hindu religion—anyone should be allowed to read the holy scriptures—and words like Brahmins, Shatriyas, Vaishya, and Shudras were only references to a person's displayed level of ability. Sarasvati believed these names for castes should not be used to designate birth status.

Sarasvati did not believe in tolerance of other religions. He claimed that other faiths were merely contaminations of the true monotheism of the *Vedas*. He considered conversions to other religions, especially to Christianity, to be intolerable. Sarasvati exerted considerable energy in converting people back to Hinduism, and even converting non-Hindus to his society. His society, the Arya Samaj, was bitterly hostile to foreign cultural influences. Sarasvati fought the resurgent Muslim movements of the mid-nineteenth century and strongly opposed the missionary activities of Christians.

Though the activities of the Arya Samaj focused on restoring early Hinduism, many of their social reforms of the Arya Samaj were undertaken as a result of Western influence. The society opposed caste based on birth, untouchability (a belief that people who performed certain menial tasks were impure, polluted, untouchable, and therefore the lowest of the Hindu caste system), ritual washings, child marriage, polygamy, and sati. In addition, the society promoted the education of women and acknowledged intercaste marriages.

Even today, the followers of Arya Samaj tend toward glory of Hinduism. For example, Arya Samaj scholars find references in the *Vedas* suggesting that thousands of years ago, Hindus were already acquainted with supposedly modern inventions such as the steam engine, the airplane, and the telegraph. Although some of Arya Samaj's ideas about technological inventions sound far-fetched, the society has been influential in ending many of the social abuses that had crept into the Hindu religion.

Ramakrishna (1836-1886)

Ramakrishna was born in Bengal into the family of a village priest. While very young, he served as a *pujari* (priest) in a temple of the goddess Kali where his older brother was the chief priest. From the age of seven, he experienced mystic trances and divine visions. Longing for an immediate experience of the divine, he often meditated before the image of Kali—the great mother goddess in her terrible form—imagining that it was breathing and listening to him. One day, while in a state of trance, Ramakrishna believed that Kali revealed herself to him. From that time on, the sight of her image or the sound of her name was enough to send him into a trance.

During the next twelve years, Ramakrishna devoted himself to the life of an ascetic, meditating and praying in a nearby forest. There he came into contact with a Kali devotee from whom he learned *sadhanas* (magical techniques) and yogic practices. Ramakrishna became a meditating yogi, worshiped like a Bhakti devotee, and explored Buddhism and Shaktism (worship of the great goddess Shakti).

Ramakrishna's visions included not only Kali, but Shiva, Rama, and Krishna. From his experiences, he believed that all religions were glorifications of the same entity. With this concept in mind, he tried to give himself visions of Muhammad and Christ. First, undertaking Islamic disciplines with a Muslim saint, he claimed to have seen Muhammad. Then he read the Bible and meditated on pictures of the Madonna and Child until the vision of Christ appeared to him. Finally, he declared that all religions were equally effective ways of reaching divinity: "As one and the same fish may be made to taste differently by different styles of cooking, so God may be enjoyed differently by his devotees."

Ramakrishna was familiar with the religious organization of Brahmo Samaj and had made friends with Keshab Chandra Sen. An organized group of disciples gathered around him during the last six years of his life, led by a young law student named Vivekananda who later became his successor.

Vivekananda (1863-1902)

Vivekananda led the Ramakrishna movement after Ramakrishna's death. When Vivekananda met his teacher, he was planning to study law in England, but within one year he had changed his mind. He became an ascetic and practiced the yogic discipline for twelve years. He was the spokesman for Hinduism at the Parliament of Religions in Chicago in 1893, where he made a great impression by stating, "All religions are one." Vivekananda founded the Vedanta Society in New York. He traveled and lectured in America and England and then returned to India. He dedicated the rest of his life to social work, particularly to the relief of poverty and to religious education, asking young men to devote themselves to uplifting the poor and starving millions.

A marked result of his success was a revival of interest in Hinduism throughout the world. Hinduism was no longer a shame-faced tradition—it had become a revitalized religion with a new sense of social conscience and nationalist fervor. Vivekananda taught that it was one of the oldest and purest religions in the world.

Rabindranath Tagore (1861-1941)

Tagore was the fourteenth of the fifteen children of Debendranath Tagore, a leading member of Brahmo Samaj. Rabindranath grew to manhood in a highly cultured family environment but did not go to school. He started writing verse from the time he was thirteen, and at twenty, he published his first volume of Bengali poems. Year after year, his writing matured in style and grew richer in content. After the death of his wife and three of his five children, Tagore published *Gitanjali* (Song Offering) in 1912. A year later, he surprised India and the world when he won the Nobel prize in literature.

■ *Ravindranath Tagore with his daughter in Rumania. Tagore wrote in English as well as in Bengali. He rejected the Hindu idea of world as illusion (**Maya**). His poems celebrate the beauties and bounties of nature and human freedom.*

Tagore founded a school in Bengal at Shantiniketan, a rural retreat, where creative and performing artists could thrive. In 1921, he expanded the retreat into a university, dedicating it to his ideal of world brotherhood and cultural interchange. Tagore loved to travel to different countries. He denounced nationalism and materialism as great evils. He believed that humanity could save itself by returning to the spiritual values that permeate all religions. Although he stressed India's role as spiritual teacher of the world, he constantly reminded his compatriots of the West's vitality and dedicated search for truth.

Once, when he returned to India from a tour of various European countries, he became aware of a new movement that had been begun by Mohandas Gandhi—a movement of noncooperation with every aspect of British influence, including the prevailing form of English education. Tagore strongly opposed Gandhi. He differed greatly from Gandhi in his attitude toward the social and ethical problems of the Hindus. He believed that politics distracted people from more important issues, such as erasing caste barriers, uplifting the poor and helpless, liberating people's minds and bodies from unnecessary burdens, and reconciling Hindus and Muslims.

Mohandas Karamchand Gandhi (1869-1949)

Today, Mohandas Karamchand Gandhi is revered by the people of India as the father of their nation. He was a great reformer, known for his nonviolent resistance methods that helped to free India from British rule. In spite of their ideological differences, Rabindranath Tagore was the first one to call Gandhi *Mahatma*, "the Great Soul."

Gandhi was born into a merchant-class family on October 2, 1869, in Porbandar Gujarat, India. As a young child, he was very shy. When he was thirteen years old, his parents arranged a marriage for him according to custom.

Later, Gandhi studied law in London and returned to India in 1891 to practice. Finding little success there, he went to British-controlled South Africa in 1893. There he experienced firsthand the prejudices held by white South Africans against Indians who claimed their rights.

Although he was to stay with his legal assignment for only one year, Gandhi remained in South Africa, working for Indian rights for the next twenty-one years. While there, he edited a newspaper called *Indian Opinion* and led many Indian-rights campaigns for which he was often arrested by the British. During these campaigns, Gandhi incorporated original ideas about what he called *satyagraha*—nonviolent social action. Satyagraha allowed people to behave with honor based on the principles of truth, nonviolence, and courage. Gandhi believed that, with satyagraha, people could act honorably in the face of injustice to bring about significant social reform.

During the twenty-one years Gandhi lived in South Africa, his own religious and ethical beliefs evolved. He was impressed by the writings of Leo Tolstoy, which planted in his mind the seeds of achieving peaceful rule through nonviolent methods. His study of the *Bhagavad Gita* and the *Sermon on the Mount* (from the Christian Bible) led him to believe that an ideal life was full of selfless action in service to fellow humans. Gandhi taught that the best way to put wrong-doers to shame was to protest without harming them. By the time he returned to India in 1915, Gandhi had decided to fight for the freedom of his native land and put an end to British rule.

Within five years of his return, Gandhi had become the leader of the Indian nationalist movement. In 1919, he used his concept of satyagraha to defeat British attempts at stifling Indian resistance. Then on April 13 of that year, in the northern state of Amritsar, an incident occurred that convinced Gandhi to develop his method of nonviolent action further—a British general ordered his soldiers to fire on an unarmed crowd. They killed almost four hundred Indians in what has come to be known as the Amritsar Massacre.

Gandhi started a national program of spinning and weaving, which he believed would help the struggle for independence by making India more self-sufficient through the dignity of labor. He hand-wove his own loin cloth and simple dress, and followed a strict vegetarian diet. Because he had given up worldly attachments, poor people trusted him unquestioningly. His ascetic temperament and his devotion to India's downtrodden poor impressed both established leaders and younger patriots. By 1920, he was the unchallenged master of the Indian Congress. Many Indians came to perceive the half-naked, bespectacled figure of Gandhi as an incarnation of the god Vishnu. Others believed him to be a great holy person who was divinely inspired.

In 1930, Gandhi led hundreds of his people in nonviolent action to protest the British Salt Acts, which required that a person buy salt only from the government. Gandhi and his followers marched two hundred miles to the sea, where they made their own salt from seawater. Gandhi continued to struggle for India's independence, and in 1942, he was jailed for the last time. This brought his accrued jail-time for political activity to seven years. Though he had been imprisoned, he believed that his actions were honorable because they had been for the common good.

Gandhi's method of nonviolence and noncooperation with British rule resulted in independence for India in 1947. However, freedom came with partition of the homeland Gandhi had worked so hard to unite. British India was divided into the two states of India and Pakistan, and with this separation came warfare between Hindus and Muslims. Gandhi deeply grieved the partition and the war, and on January 13, 1948, he began a fast, hoping to convince people to end the bloodshed and live together in peace. By January eighteenth, Hindu and Muslim leaders agreed to stop fighting, and Gandhi broke his fast. But just twelve days later in New Delhi, Gandhi was assassinated by an orthodox Hindu who feared the Mahatma's tolerance for all creeds and religions.

Gandhi truly believed in simple living and high thinking. He followed the path of orthodox Hinduism. Throughout his life he had two dimensions, one religious and the other political. While his religion inspired him to seek perfection and purity, his political dimension led him to emphasize practical solutions. Thus he was able to activate effectively the old principle of *ahimsa*—nonviolence—in contemporary politics.

Vinoba Bhave (1895-1970)

Gandhi emphasized that truth and nonviolence could resolve a variety of human problems. One of the major figures who followed these principles was Vinoba Bhave. Bhave's parents wanted their son to pursue higher education in England. Instead, he burned his important school certificates and joined Gandhi's ashram (religious community) in Gujarat. There he led an austere life, working side by side with Gandhi to achieve independence.

Ghandi's successor in the area of politics was Jawaharlal Nehru. After Gandhi's assassination, however, Bhave was seen as the Mahatma's heir to the realm of nonviolent theory and practice. Beginning in 1951, Bhave conceptualized and developed a movement of voluntary land donations. The movement's vision of India was that of a nation with a network of self-sufficient communities. Bhave begged rich landowners to donate land for religious and ethical principles. Landowners donated over four million acres, which Bhave distributed to farmers who had no land of their own.

The modern saints of Hinduism, from Rammohan Roy to Mahatma Gandhi, have done tremendous work to reform the internal abuses of Hinduism. The efforts of these modern saints were enhanced by Hinduism's remarkable ability to adapt to changing times. Hinduism does not have an unbendable doctrinal shell; there has always been room for change. Because of the open-ended nature of this religion, saints continue to appear, and there is constant discussion and revision. Old traditions are revitalized, and if need be, new ideas integrated and new religious societies begun. Freedom of individual thought has been intrinsically sacred to Hinduism and made all innovations possible.

CHAPTER **6**

The Hindu Temple, Icons, and Worship

*T*he Hindu temple is known by many different names, three of which are *mandira* (waiting place), *prasada* (seat), and *devalaya* (house of god). However, the most popular term for the Hindu temple is *mandira*. The mandira is believed to be the earthly seat of a deity and the place where deities wait for their devotees. The belief that goddesses and gods dwell in the mandira can be traced as far as the epics and the *Puranas*.

In later sacred texts such as the *Shastras*, special chapters were written about the building of a mandira. In these texts, the mandira is described as a crossing place where worlds of divinity and humanity meet. Hindus believe that a deity descends to earth and takes form through sacred images located in the mandira. Some believe that by seeing (Darshana) and touching the image, it is possible to ascend temporarily to heaven and experience the divine. Although Hindus believe that God is found everywhere in the world, they also believe that their respect for the divine world, displayed in the symbolism found throughout the mandira, helps give shape to a divine reality that would otherwise remain formless.

In order to understand how a temple becomes a place in which deity and humankind meet, it is necessary to grasp the symbolic meaning not only of the Hindu mandira but also of pilgrimage centers (*tirtha sthana*), sacred images or icons (*murti*), the way of worship (*puja*), the worshiper (*pujak*), and the nature of sacred Hindu texts.

The Hindu Mandira

From the early Vedic period, Hindus have tried to create a sacred space to which gods could descend and partake of human offerings, and in which people could be with the gods or ascend toward the heavens. During the later Vedic period, prayers were conveyed to the gods through sacrificial fires believed to be manifestations of Agni, the god of fire. Through fires, Vedic priests "ascended" to heaven. All such rites and ceremonies were performed in a sacred enclosure specifically prepared for the communion. The tradition of this symbolic meeting of the human and the divine continues today in the Hindu mandira.

A mandira is constructed according to specific requirements. The site for a mandira is carefully selected. Brahmanic texts called *Shilpa Shastras*, written to direct architects and artisans, describe the requirements for such a site. One *Purana* adds to the ideas about how to build a temple with a verse. It says that "the gods always play where groves are near rivers, mountains, and springs and in towns with pleasure gardens. . . . It is such places that the gods love and always dwell in."

When a site has been selected, local spirits of the land are driven away before construction begins. Then the ground is plowed and several seeds are sown. By observing the quality of the newborn plants, the builder determines the quality of the soil. Next, the earth is smoothed until it is perfectly even, like a mirror. On this prepared land a circle is drawn, symbolizing heaven, and a square is drawn around the circle, symbolizing earth. It is believed that the center of this circle forms a sacred pillar, connecting the "body" of the mandira with heaven. A small chest holding jewels and seeds and representing the essence of the temple is buried in the ground near the pillar. Above this, the innermost sanctuary, the *garbhagrah*, or "womb chamber," is constructed.

Motifs of mountains and caves are often incorporated skillfully into the architecture of the Hindu mandira. Throughout Hindu mythology, mountains have been depicted as sacred. Mount Kailasha in the Himalayas is the abode of Shiva; Mount Meru, like a Hindu mandira, is believed to be the axis of the universe, joining celestial, atmospheric, and terrestrial regions. In fact, the superstructure of a Hindu temple is called *shikhara,* meaning "the top of a mountain." Caves are also important natural symbols in Hinduism because as dark chambers with one small opening, they are believed to be symbolic of and imbued with the spirituality of the maternal womb. These chambers have traditionally served as ascetic retreats.

There are two kinds of mandira: rock-cut cave shrines and temples with towers. Many Hindu texts explain these symbols of cave (the inner sanctuary) and mountain (the superstructure of the mandira). However, during the epic and Puranic periods, the Bhakti movement that emphasized devotional worship was the major influence on such temple building and the dedication of many temples to personal gods.

The earliest examples of Hindu temples were constructed around the fifth century C.E. These early stone temples were simple, columned halls covered with a flat roof. Later, this form developed into a square-columned hall raised on a flat, broad *bhumi,* or base, (literally translated as "earth") that led to the superstructure, a tower. The tower, or shikhara ("the mountain peak"), was one of the most important parts of the mandira.

The shikhara rose at the rear of the mandira. It marked the location of the interior garbhagrah where the deity was believed to be enshrined. Divine light was believed to emit from this small, dark chamber and bless, protect, and watch over the community. Around this innermost shrine was a passageway on which devotees, moving clockwise, could encircle the inner chamber. The garbhagrah had just one opening and only the presiding priest was allowed inside.

An assembly hall, the *mandapa,* was located in the sanctuary. This hall often led to another hall, the *natya mandapa,* where dances were performed and hymns sung to please the deities. These halls opened onto a veranda, which led to the outside.

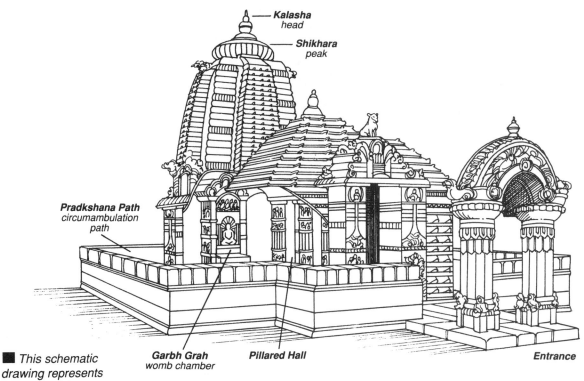

Kalasha
head

Shikhara
peak

Pradkshana Path
circumambulation
path

Garbh Grah
womb chamber

Pillared Hall

Entrance

■ *This schematic drawing represents the essential parts of a Hindu temple.*

The outer surface of the temple held detailed sculptures. Mythological scenes were depicted, juxtaposed with scenes from everyday life or important political events such as a royal coronation, conquests and celebrations, or portraits of royal and secular patrons. The main gateway leading toward the inner sanctuary was the only opening between sacred and profane spaces. Other openings—doors, niches, and windows—were architectural symbols of the passage of humanity to God.

The mandira has always been the focus of the religious, social, and cultural life of the Hindus. However, during Hindu rule it was also the political and economic center. Many features of the mandira have remained the same, both structurally and functionally.

By the eighth century, many freestanding temples were carved from gigantic, solid stone hills. One of these was the Shiva temple at Ellora (in the state of Maharashtra). Other sacred temples with detailed mythological scenes were carved in and around immense caves, such as Elephanta (in Maharashtra) and Mahaballipuram (in Tamil Nadu). These elaborate temple complexes were sculptural and architectural marvels.

Many temple complexes resembled palace architecture. This is not surprising given that deities were considered kings. The earthly kings, who were mandira patrons, were considered to be divine reflections who watched over the welfare of their kingdoms. In some texts, kings were described as supports or receptacles of gods. Sometimes, kings were believed to be intermediaries between earth and heaven, transmitting the offerings of their subjects to the celestial region and bringing back divine blessings. At times, kings were believed to be incarnations of deities or even demons, depending on the nature of their reign and protection. The royal throne was often equated with the altar, and conversely, the temple was perceived as a divine fortress from which the deities protected the world from chaos and disorder.

The mandira has always been a nucleus around which all artistic, intellectual, and religious life of the Hindu community was centered. Dance, music, drama, art, and architecture, were integral parts of the mandira rituals. Thus, sacred dances and dramas were performed in the assembly halls. Mythological stories, recited earlier by bards, were enacted in the mandira. Worshipers sang devotional songs and recited hymns from important scriptures, such as the *Vedas,* and the *Puranas,* and the epics.

During celebrations and festivals, money, land, or valuable objects were donated to the mandira by kings and rich patrons of the kingdom. Some kings in southern India celebrated battle victories or the addition of a territory to their kingdom by bestowing magnificent gifts on the mandira. Inscriptions on the walls of these temples describe priceless necklaces of lustrous pearls and bright coral beads, as well as gold ornaments set in precious stones. These were donated to adorn the sacred images in the temples. Utensils of pure gold were given for daily services to the deities, and metal images of the most popular divinities—Nataraja, Vishnu, Rama, Krishna, Shiva and Parvati—were presented to the temple.

Temple building and the installation of sacred images was not only an expression of devotion and piety but also a merit-gaining act, or an act of good karma. All donor-devotees were promised peace, wealth, grain, and sons if they erected a temple or donated an icon. In addition, the generous gifts demonstrated physical importance and economic power to subjects and neighboring rulers.

Today, the Hindu mandira is considered a holy place in the midst of a profane world. As they always have been, temples and shrines are considered earthly dwelling places of the deities and a "crossing" where devotees of any caste can be with the divine reality. In a temple, worshipers believe that they can leave the world of illusion behind and approach the eternal realm of knowledge and truth.

■ *Reliefs and sculptures decorate the outer walls of major Hindu temples. These works bring the mythological stories and their characters to life in exquisite detail.*

All Hindu communities have one or more local temples. Some are monumental, some are of average size, and some are quite small. Large temples are always devoted to one of the manifestations of the major deities like Shiva, Vishnu, or some form of Devi. The smaller temples are devoted to minor regional deities known only to the local people. Hindus believe that they are linked with the sacred through these large temples and small shrines.

Tirtha

Like Hindu temples, *tirtha sthana* (pilgrimage centers) are crossing places of the earthly and the spiritual worlds. *Tirtha* literally means a "crossing place" or a "ford," and in a tirtha, worshipers feel closer to or even united with the deities. Journeying to a tirtha became popular because it was considered as beneficial to the pilgrim as Vedic sacrifices were to a Brahmin. Moreover, tirtha participation was accessible to devotees of all castes.

In these pilgrimage centers, worshipers have access to the mythical personages, gods, goddesses, and saints who were either born or incarnated, and who performed feats of austerity at these particular sites. People travel to far-off centers because they believe that the holy places radiate sacredness for the benefit of devotees. At the holy sites, devotees feel closer to the sacred events that took place there and feel as though they were participating in the sacred history.

Several tirtha sthana are scattered throughout India. However, four are particularly important: Badrinath in the northern Himalayas; Puri in the east; Ramesvaram in the south; and Dvarka in the west. By visiting all these sacred places one after another, in clockwise order, pilgrims encircle the holy land of India. This is just like the journey made when walking around the innermost sanctum of a mandira. Walking around the sanctum is considered an important ritual and a form of communion with God.

Most tirtha sthana are located in places that are difficult to reach. They are on the tops of mountains, deep in forests, or in the middle of deserts. Most are not accessible by modern transportation. To reach the holy destination, pilgrims need self-discipline, endurance, and devotion. A pilgrim's effort is comparable to the austerities of an ascetic, and from it, Hindus believe that they gain spiritual merit. In addition, a person may gain status in his community after having returned from a pilgrimage.

Hindus compare their life from birth to death to a pilgrim's journey with many stations. They do not consider death as final destination but as just one station in an endless cycle of lives. Nor do Hindus believe that death automatically brings liberation from the frustrations of life. Rather, they believe that moksha (final release) can be attained by complete devotion to God, knowledge of God, and through good works. Those who cannot liberate their atman (individual soul) through any of these means might attain it by completing a pilgrimage. Pilgrimage brings spiritual joy and ultimate release from the world. By visiting a tirtha sthana, a devotee not only recreates and participates in sacred history by being at the site of some mythological incident—but he or she is also able to visit the temples of these places that are charged with intense sacredness.

Hindu Icons

In the Sanskrit language, a sacred statue is called *murti*. The term, which is more than two thousand years old, refers to any figure that has a definite shape. Hindu icons, or sacred images, may be anthropomorphic—having human likeness—or they may be abstract. From the terra-cotta figurines of the Indus valley to the modern images of Durga, all murtis are considered genuinely sacred.

The word *murti* is used in the *Upanishads* and the *Bhagavad Gita*, and it implies much more than just a simple statue. Hindu icons visually express an invisible yet fantastic divine reality. For example, the head of Nataraja, the four arms of Vishnu, Ganesha's elephant head, or Skanda's six heads are all fantastic forms depicting an incomprehensible reality. As sacred statues, these forms are easier for humankind to understand.

When icons are seen as personal deities, such as in the worship of a Bhakti, they are considered to be charged with the presence of the god. Worshiping an image is one of the ways in which a devotee can gain access to a deity. The god is invited, bathed, adorned, touched, seen, and honored in the form of the murti, or sacred image. Therefore, deep respect for the image of a goddess or god allows people to show their deep love for that goddess or god. Through the image, devotees can pour their emotions to the deity.

The *Shilpa Shastras* are texts that give detailed descriptions of how a sacred image ought to be created and made suitable for the presence of a deity. The texts provide measurements of body parts, the correct posture, number of hands and heads, hand gestures (*mudras*), emblems and weapons to be held, the appropriate *vahana* (animal vehicle), suitable seat (*asana*), and more. An image must be proportionate, technically correct, and pleasing to the eye. Only then do Hindus believe that it will be fit for a deity's residence. Such specific details of the gods are the result of meditation, experimentation, and extreme devotion by generations of priests and artists.

In addition to the size, shape, and artistic quality of a murti, there are many rituals that govern its actual making. First, whether an icon is made from wood or stone, it is important for the shilpin, or sculptor, to follow the advice of a Brahmin and cut the tree or quarry the stone at the proper time and in the proper manner. Because Hindus believe that each and every grain of matter is inhabited by local spirits, part of the ritual includes asking the spirits of the tree or rock to leave and dwell elsewhere. It is important to have a "clean" block of raw material, free of all spirits, on which to carve a divine image.

To make the icon, shilpins read about the image in the *Shilpa Shastras*. Then they focus mentally until they can form an image of the icon. Before starting the work, a ritual purification must be performed. Thus, for a traditional image-maker, creating an icon is equivalent to yogic discipline in that it requires intense meditation.

When an image is completed, special rites of blessing take place. The image is purified with a variety of ritual substances such as clarified butter, honey, and a special kind of grass. In particular, the eyes of the deity are sealed with the honey and butter. Then a priest installs various deities in different parts of the body of the icon by touching its individual parts. With this

■ *Ganesha, the elephant-headed son of Shiva, is the god of beginnings. Devotees worship him in order to overcome difficulties in completing a task. Ganesha blesses devotees and removes obstacles.*

ritual, a particular icon may be symbolically inhabited by a number of gods other than that which it depicts. Having many gods in one recalls the one body of the Vedic Primal Man (Purusha) and the deities created from it in the Vedic hymn, *Purusha Shukta*.

Finally, breath is infused in the image through a rite called *pratishtha*, meaning "establishing the breathlike." During this rite, a special *mantra* (secret verse) is uttered. Then, the eyes are opened with a golden needle. After the blessing, the icon is considered suitable for the deity to descend to temporarily. Most of the images are established in this manner to invoke the presence of a deity. Without the complex rituals of purification and the rites of establishment, icons are plain works of art with no sacred power.

Icons of a deity rarely show the god in one form. Rather, gods and goddesses are shown in their numerous manifestations. For instance, Shiva is depicted as Nataraja or with Parvati. Vishnu is shown in his various incarnations—Krishna, Rama, Kalki, and others. Krishna and Durga are sculpted as slaying their enemies in violent and terrifying postures.

■ The center of attention during the **Durga Puja** celebration is the image of the goddess **Mahishamardini**, "the slayer of the demon Mahisha." Each year, at the end of the celebration, the image of the goddess is immersed in water.

A mandira has movable and immovable murtis. Immovable images are part of the temple architecture, whereas movable images can be taken out during festival days for "seeing" the deities. *Darshana*, or seeing images of deities, becomes a significant act whether a deity is at home, at the temple, or journeying in a procession. This rite of seeing is one of the basic components of Hindu worship.

Puja

Daily worship, *puja,* is an important ritual in the lives of practicing Hindus. The daily rituals performed in the mandira are thought to be a source of prosperity and good health for the worshiper. The goal of puja is reminiscent of the Vedic fire sacrifice, in which gods were invited from the heavens and presented with different offerings. Puja is the most frequently performed Hindu ritual.

Vedic people believed that deities lived in the heavens. By the epic period, it was believed that divine power came to earth if a sacred area was made ritually pure, icons were consecrated, and the deity was persuaded with verbal chants to descend. Then the god or goddess was given constant love and honor. This was because the early Hindus believed that if proper devotion and care were given to the invited deity, it would stay in the temple and watch over the community. If proper care of the images was not taken, and if the icons were not protected from vandalism and abuse, the deity would abandon it and the temple.

The idea of constant attention to a deity made it necessary for a daily routine of rituals. This resulted in the development of the Hindu puja. In each mandira, a resident priest makes sure that at sunrise, noon, sunset, and midnight the proper puja is performed. In addition, the priest resides in the temple so that continuous care may be taken and the god will always be present.

Visiting a mandira every day or even regularly is not mandatory for Hindus. Many devout Hindus keep in touch with their deities through worship at home. However, some rituals cannot be performed at home and a priest's assistance is needed.

Puja is not congregational worship but an individual offering to one deity or to a deity and his or her companion. Reasons for temple worship could be related to personal or family health, wealth, education, general blessings, or safety. Many strive for good karma or liberation (mukti). Present-day rituals of puja, at home and in the temple, have not altered much from what was practiced during the earliest periods, although the ancient rituals have been greatly simplified.

Puja consists of three ritual steps: first, seeing the deity (darshana); second, puja, or worship, which includes offering flowers, fruits and cooked food called *bhog;* and third, retrieving the blessed food, called *prasada,* and consuming it. By these sacred acts, Hindus create a relationship with the divinity through their emotions and senses. As one scholar writes, "The temple is the monument of (divine) manifestations. The devotee who comes to the temple to look at it, does so as a seer, not as a mere spectator."

In their homes, most Hindus keep a shrine dedicated to one or more deities. The shrine contains images of the family deity, major gods and goddesses, saints, and ancestors. It is kept in a sacred area—which may be a corner of a room, a niche, a shelf of a cabinet or, in an affluent household, a small room set aside solely for this purpose. Other ritual paraphernalia include a container of water for sprinkling and purifying the area, a bell, a lamp to be waved in front of the deity, an incense burner, and a tray with flowers, fruit, and freshly cooked food. At the household shrine, Hindus offer a simple daily puja.

During the puja, the head of a Hindu household invites the goddess or god to descend and be present at the ceremony. When the divine presence is felt, worshipers consider that the deity has entered the murti, and they offer it a seat, wash its feet, and give water to it. An image might be symbolically bathed, then clothed in new garments and embellished with ornaments. Perfumes and ointments are applied, flowers and garlands are placed in before it. Incense is burned, and a burning lamp is waved in front of the deity. Foods such as cooked rice, fruit, butter, and sugar are offered. Family members bow before the image, sip the blessed water, and receive a portion of the cooked food, which, having been blessed by the deity, is now considered prasada for the devotees. Finally, the deity is asked to rest or depart.

*In Hindu homes, **Puja** is part of the day-to-day routine. Here a woman is preparing to pray in front of her home shrine, installed in front of a window. Notice the flower garlands, bell, vessels, and other **Puja** ingredients.*

In the home, the deities are invited to descend. In the mandira, on the other hand, they are "awakened," because in the temple, the divine guests are in their earthly home. The gods are believed to dwell in the mandira as royalty. At the mandira, full puja is performed several times every day. It differs from the daily puja performed at a home more in scale than in substance. In the temples that enshrine major Brahmanic gods, priests are referred to as Brahmins. Smaller temples and shrines of minor deities may be presided over by a member of a lower caste.

The light within a mandira is dim, caressing the eye of a devotee who may have come in from bright light. The *mandapa* (assembly hall) is charged with the scent of flowers, burning oil lamps, and incense. A devotee walks slowly toward the innermost sanctuary of the deity with the ingredients for puja, which may include flowers, fruit, and cooked bhog. Near the sanctuary, these things are handed to the priest, who then performs puja on behalf of the worshiper.

After seeing the image and receiving the prasada, the devotee walks around the passageway of the sanctuary. The ritual of *pradikshana*—encircling the womb chamber clockwise and touching the outer walls of the innermost sanctuary—is an important part of the mandira ritual that cannot be performed at home. Walking around an image, the inner sanctum, or the mandira itself, is a way of paying respect to the deity, for movement is considered an important part of puja.

In addition to prayers and offerings, Hindu worship includes an understanding of the godly image, an experience charged with religious meaning. This experience is encouraged by the ancient act of "seeing." It is not only the worshiper "seeing" the image but also the deity "seeing" the worshiper that is considered a favorable act. This act is called Darashana. For this reason, Hindu images have strikingly large eyes to facilitate the "exchange of glances" between devotee and deity.

Similarly, in puja one does not only see but touches and hears as well. All the senses are given special significance in puja. One observes the offering of the lighted lamps, touches the ritual objects and feet of the deity (where possible), hears the ringing of the bells and the sacred sounds being recited, smells the incense, and tastes the blessed food offered at the end of the ritual.

The Worshiper

A Hindu worshiper, or *pujak*, may perform daily puja at home and on special days in the mandira. Pujaks must be physically healthy as well as ritually clean before starting to worship. They must take a bath, wear fresh clothes, and free their minds of any impure thoughts. A priest must also be physically and ritually clean. Through purifying acts, priests and worshipers are able to identify themselves with the divine object of worship.

In worship, devotees see divine images and mythological scenes on the outer walls of the mandira. These help the worshipers to recall all the sacred stories they have heard about or read. With their minds full of the stories and their senses full from worship, devotees believe that they come to know that which is unknowable. Through art, architectural forms, and devotion, the worshiper can find new spiritual meaning in things.

The doorway of the mandira is believed to be vulnerable to the evils of the outside world. Therefore, minor divinities such as door guardians and images of sacred rivers are carved on or placed near lintels and doorjambs. These images are thought to cleanse devotees of any mental or physical impurities. They also bestow divine blessings on them as they enter the mandira.

Inside the mandira, worshipers are said to move toward the divine. They walk through a series of enclosures that become increasingly more sacred. As a person passes through these enclosures, he or she is gradually raised from an earthly level to a sacred level.

In the mandira, the worshipers do not physically ascend to heaven. However, by focusing spiritually, they may gain a divine enlightenment. From open spaces they reach closed spaces; from light they enter darkness; from the complexity of the world they move to the simplicity of the divine. In the final stage, the worshipers approach the doorway of the garbhagrah (womb chamber) and hand their offerings to the priest, who then conducts puja for them. The devotee waits outside, following the movements of the priest.

A common part of Hindu worship is the gestures of humility such as bowing, kneeling, lying prostrate, and the touching of feet. Honor and affection are expressed by doing for the god what one does daily for cherished family members. Family activities such as waking, bathing, dressing, cooking, serving, and sleeping become refined by daily practice. Hindu puja consists of doing these day-to-day activities to honor personal gods. Mundane daily acts, when refined, become ritual acts fit to be performed for the family deity. Finally, at the special time of puja, the god is invited, bathed, adorned, touched, seen, and honored. The secular feelings become charged with sacred intensity. Human feelings become divine love. Thus the family relationships and ritual acts of puja are closely interwoven. Routine chores become sacred rites when performed in honor of a deity.

CHAPTER 7

Social Duty and Rites of Passage

*D*harma, meaning moral duty or law, is an important term in Hinduism. The origin and meaning of this word goes back as far as the Vedic period, when the word *rita* meant cosmic order. According to the divine law of rita, all things in the world have a proper place, function, and order. This creates a balance in the universe.

In Vedic times, cosmic order included the duty to be moral. In the *Shastra* texts, the idea of rita branched into the concepts of dharma. In those texts, dharma not only meant cosmic law and moral duty but also social, ethical, and religious duty. *Shastras* emphasize that the reality of the universe depends on the proper behavior of the people. An improper action, that is, *adharma*, can lead to the fall of the universe into unreality and eventually into nothingness. Therefore, in order to maintain the universe and enhance cosmic harmony, proper behavior is necessary. Dharma, then, is responsible for the maintenance of the Hindu world.

In Hinduism, the moral and social duties of dharma are tied to the theories of karma, samsara, and ultimately, moksha. Therefore, it is important to learn about these three terms before

discussing Hindu *varnasramadharma*, a system of duty or law that includes the four castes and the four stages of life.

Origins of Dharma

The ideas of ethical behavior and moral life come from sacred Hindu literature. Traditionally, Hindu literature has been divided into two classes. One class is *shruti* ("what is heard"), covering the *Vedas* and *Upanishads*. The other is *smriti* ("what is remembered"), covering the epics and *Puranas*. The smriti literature also includes a new literary form called *sutras*.

The sutras provided moral teachings. The word *sutra* literally means "a thread," and its content was to be memorized in addition to the *Vedas*. The earliest of the sutras were the *Griha Sutras* (domestic rituals) and *Srauta Sutras* (priestly rituals). The last of the series were compositions called *Dharma Sutras* (ways of moral behavior).

The sutras were written by the Brahmins before the beginning of the present era. It perhaps seemed to the later Vedic Brahmins that one's religious life should be concerned with more than rituals—their texts describe how leading an ethical life is an integral part of religious life. The Brahmins do not deny that the rituals are sacred, but they stress the importance of ethical behavior, give instructions in social duty, and teach sacred morality. Their texts were called *dharmasutras*.

Dharmasutras were difficult to understand. Therefore, these texts were explained and expanded into compositions called *Dharma Shastras*. The Shastras were written in verse, and they were easier to memorize and grasp than the Dharmasutras. Eventu-ally, Hindus turned to the *Dharma Shastras* as guides to ideal social behavior.

The most influential of all the *Dharma Shastras* was written by a sage named Manu. This text, written some time between 200 B.C.E. and 200 C.E., is known as the *Laws of Manu*. The *Laws of Manu* seems to have established the public norm of today's Hindu society.

The *Dharma Shastras* say that those who support dharma gain fame while alive and incomparable happiness after death. To support dharma is to behave in an ethical manner. The term *dharma*, therefore, is closely related to the idea of karma—that one's actions in the present determine the conditions of one's life in the future.

Karma and Samsara

Originally, any correct activity or properly performed ritual was called *karma*. However, later religious philosophers expanded the meaning of this term. It came to mean that one's present actions determine one's future life. Thus, underlying the Hindu law of karma is the idea that a person's behavior leads to an appropriate reward or punishment.

Some scholars think that the idea that a future life depended on previous behavior must have developed from a long period of keenly observing plants, trees, and fields. These scholars believe that the early Hindus noted that land "gives birth" repeatedly if healthy seeds are sown and tended. They saw that plants do not really die; the death of a plant is a process by which it renews itself in the spring. In a sense, each life of a plant ends in a death in order to be reborn. A plant's regrowth is determined by the healthy or unhealthy conditions of former births. Scholars believe the early Hindus felt the same to be true of all living things.

During the Vedic period, proper ritual performance was called karma. In that era, if a priest performed certain rituals correctly he was believed to control the gods. Later, Upanishadic seers taught our current understanding of karma. They believed that all physical and mental activity was a reflection of greater cosmic processes. They taught that a person becomes good through good actions and bad through bad actions. Through these seers, the concept of the cycles of life, death, rebirth, and redeath was reinforced. These cycles were called *samsara*.

The theories of karma and samsara provide Hindus with a reason for human differences. If people are of differing social classes or physical and mental abilities, it must be a result of their deeds in this life or a past life. Karma and samsara also encourage Hindus to act ethically, because if they do not, they will suffer for their poor actions in the future.

The samsara cycles are an ever-changing universe of requirements, consequences, and conditions. This universe contrasts with the unconditioned and eternal world of the gods. The goal of practicing Hindus is to liberate themselves from constantly changing samsara—to find release from the cycles of rebirths and redeaths and gain existence in the realm of the gods.

Moksha

Moksha is the release from the conditional and temporary existence of this world. It is a religious state for which every Hindu strives. Moksha cannot be gained by action aimed at achieving something in this world. Rather, the person who wants liberation from life—*mukti*—seeks to experience the oneness of *atman-Brahman*, the union of one's self with the Ultimate Reality.

Moksha is not a Vedic concept. The Vedic texts are concerned with enjoyment of earthly bounties. Vedic people were awed by natural powers. They composed and chanted hymns to appease the personifications of natural forces and invite these personified gods to share the bounties of the earth. Vedic people did not want release from the good earthly life.

In Indian thought, the notion of moksha appeared as early as the oldest *Upanishad*. The term *moksha* is mentioned sometime during the sixth century C.E., and the concept is elaborated on in the epic *Mahabharata* and the *Dharma Shastras*.

A Hindu is supposed to model his life according to the dharmic norm prescribed in the Laws of Manu. He must obey caste laws and follow the stages of life. If he leads an ideal life, as described in the sacred text, he will achieve liberation. This ideal Hindu life is reflected in the model of varnasramadharma.

Varnasramadharma

Varnasramadharma is a term that combines three separate words: *varna*, meaning the social caste system; *asrama*, meaning the stages of life; and *dharma*, which means duty, law, or proper behavior. Varansramadharma is based on reciprocal social obligations. It was described in *Dharma Shastras* as a guide for male members of the Hindu community. Later, it became a system for Hindu society in general. Varnasramadharma and samsara give moral, ethical, and social values to members of the Hindu community and form the basis of the Hindu society.

The system of varnasramadharma was stimulated by the coming of outsiders. It was created to keep foreigners away from the core of society. It also served to organize the diverse occupations of Hindus and make a householders's position strong. This model evolved by combining two social ideals. The first is that of *varna*, the four hierarchical castes (Brahmins, Shatriyas, Vaishyas, and Shudras). The second is that of *asrama*, or the male member's four stages of life—*brahmachari* (student), *grahasthin* (householder), *vanaprasthin* (forest dweller), and *sanyasin* (ascetic).

Varnasramadharma is a guide to living with the laws of dharma and karma. Within this system, Hindus support each other by performing the duties of their particular varna. Hindus believe that if one person does his duty imperfectly, it harms the entire society and thus the universe as a whole. One person's dharma, or duty, cannot be performed by another. As the *Bhagavad Gita* says, "It is better to perform one's own obligations poorly than to do another's well."

As a general rule, all the important Hindu texts assert that people, regardless of their age and occupation, should observe some common moral obligations. For example, everyone must tell the truth, practice goodwill, be forgiving, and exercise patience at all times. Such rules, in addition to varnasramadharma, are called *sanatana* (eternal) or *sadharana* (pertaining to everyone). Hindus commonly call their religion *Sanatana Dharma*.

These ideals of the four castes (see page 12) and the four stages of life (see page 13) were set forth in the Hindu texts. But in practice, not many men went beyond the stage of householder. However, the possibility was open for a householder to pursue the life of a forest dweller in order to achieve moksha.

Varna

The idea that the world is balanced when it is made up of distinct social classes, or castes, is rooted in the Vedic hymn *Purusha Shukta*:

> *When they divided the Man (Purusha)*
> *into how many parts did they divide him?*
> *What was his mouth, what were his arms,*
> *What were his thighs and his feet called?*

The Brahmin was his mouth,
of his arms was made Shatriya,
his thighs became the Vaishyas,
of his feet the Shudra was born.

The *Laws of Manu* affirm that this Vedic hymn is the Hindu justification for its social system—*varna*. The hymn refers to social divisions believed to be typical of the Aryans who immigrated to the Indus Valley and eventually to the Ganges plains. These were the Vedic people. We do not have any historical record that defines varna as such, but it appears from the Vedic hymns that the social system was composed of four major subdivisions—the Brahmins, the priestly class; Shatriyas, nobles or warriors; Vaishyas, the merchants and farmers; and Shudras, the servant class.

As time passed, this system became very complex. A person's duty varied according to his caste and to the stage of life he was passing through. Moreover, an individual's sex, family, and region further complicated the matter.

At present, the varna system has developed into *jatis* (subcastes) because of inter-caste and interracial marriages. When members of the same caste married, the same caste continued for the next generation. When members of different castes married, their offspring generated a new caste. This new generation belonged to a caste lower than the three upper castes, but higher than Shudra (the lowest). However, if a member of any of the three upper classes married a Shudra or a member of any other race, their children were "untouchables." These children belonged to a class lower than the Shudras. This complicated system resulted in creation of thousands of jatis.

Hindus belonging to these jatis live throughout India. They have rules governing marriage, food, occupation, and other activities. This is done to keep family purity. Punishment for disobeying the rules of marriage results in expulsion from the jati to which one belongs.

For many Hindus, the jatis are simply subdivisions of the classical varna. Belonging to a particular varna through their jati is important because they believe that it plays a part in the reward or punishment each soul receives for its actions during a previous existence. For Hindus, present life conditions have something to do with the purity and sanctity of Brahmins and the high or low rank attributed to each jati. However, social caste is believed to be due mainly to the life led by a soul in its previous incarnations. Brahmins are supposed to have the purest souls. If a Brahmin is wicked, however, he may be reborn as a member of a much lower caste or even as an untouchable as punishment.

The four varnas make up a workable system that depicts all members of society supporting each other. Brahmins, at the top of the system, were formerly required to teach the *Vedas,* assist in sacrifices, and accept gifts. No other caste under any circumstances could perform these three duties. The top priority of the Brahmins was maintaining the purity of their class for the purpose of domestic and temple rituals. Vegetarianism was encouraged and eventually became a norm among Brahmins. Thus, Brahmins who "were not desirous of killing" retained their higher rank.

Shatriyas were rulers and warriors. As kings, they had power on earth. They protected their subjects and looked after the proper functioning of the society. As warriors, their caste duty was to slay enemies. Vaishyas, on the other hand, had the duty of breeding cattle. In addition, they were agriculturists and moneylenders. Along with Brahmins and Shatriyas, they could study the *Vedas*, perform sacrifices, and offer sacred gifts. Moreover, they, too, participated in the rites of passage and wore the sacred thread. However, the Vaishyas were not permitted to perform religious rites or the duties of a warrior.

Shudras performed only minor sacrifices and simplified domestic rituals that did not require reciting from the *Vedas*. They did all sorts of manual work so that society as a whole could function smoothly. They were not permitted to perform any sacred rituals. Furthermore, they were not officially initiated into the system of varnasramadharma, although they took care of the basic necessities of the society.

Asrama

During the sixth century , the idea of a life of celibacy and renunciation was sweeping the Ganges river valley. New religions, such as Buddhism and Jainism, had branched away from the Vedic tradition. Considering that human beings were bound to endless cycles of samsara, common people questioned the value of Vedic sacrifices. What was the purpose of the Vedic sacrificial ritual done in order to appease gods? If humans were bound to samsara no matter what, how was sacrifice going to help?

During this fertile period of varied religious growth, Brahmins attempted to find theological justifications for their way of thinking so that their members would not convert to other religions. They wanted to find a religious way that would make the life of ascetics and renouncers acceptable in the mainstream of their own religion, while still maintaining the religious importance of marriage, ritual sacrifice, and other Vedic institutions. One of their solutions was the system of the *ashramas*, which became one of the most significant of the sacred laws.

Ashramas are viewed as the four rungs in the ladder leading up to liberation, or moksha. Although the student stage is the time for preparation for adult life, the householder stage is the most important stage in this system. The forest dweller and ascetic stages are regarded as belonging to the time of old age and retirement. Persons situated in each asrama are expected to pay respect to those who belong to a higher stage than they do.

Brahmachari, the Student

As a student, or *brahmachari,* a Hindu male was to study diligently in order to know the sacred traditions and literature. Between the ages of eight and twelve, a boy of any of the three upper castes could study the *Vedas* after he was initiated by a teacher who had accepted him as a student. The boy went through a rite of initiation before he was allowed to live with his teacher. Once accepted, he was instructed in the recitation of the sacred texts.

In the teacher's ashram, the student lived a life of poverty and submission. He was supposed to live as a personal servant of the teacher and do all of his teacher's daily chores, such as toting fuel and water, serving food, and cleaning up. He was expected to show great devotion and respect to his teacher. He completed his studies after several years of living in this manner.

Grahasthin, the Householder

When the young man completed his studies, he was expected to marry. This was considered the second asrama, that of *grahasthin*, the householder. The man was expected to earn a living for himself, beget sons, and take care of his family by doing work appropriate to his caste. In addition, he was expected to give alms to those who had passed into the higher asrama, that of the forest dweller and ascetic.

Marriage and begetting sons was immensely important in this asrama. The relationship between husband and wife is described in the *Dharma Shastras.* As long as the wife lived, she was not to do anything to displease her husband. After his death, she was to remain devoted to his memory and was never to even utter the name of another man.

Vanaprahasthin, the Forest Dweller

When a man had fulfilled his duties as the head of the family, when his skin was wrinkled and his hair white, he was expected to leave his home and community and proceed toward the higher asrama—*vanaprahasthin*—that of the forest dweller. The forest dweller contributed to the welfare of the society by performing rituals in honor of his ancestors. However, only a very small percentage of people really left home in order to live in the forest away from family and community. Most people paid homage to their ancestors while living at home and went on pilgrimages each year to be closer to the gods.

Sanyasin, the Ascetic

The last asrama in one's life, sanyasa, became necessary if one wished to achieve liberation. The difference between a forest dweller and an ascetic is never clearly stated in Hindu texts. Perhaps seclusion from family and community for a period of time, that is, living the life of a forest dweller, was essential before one could completely give up the world, physically as well as mentally.

It was only at this fourth stage that one could understand the mystery of the divine, experience its presence, and possibly have communion with it. A forest dweller who was not a sanyasin

■ *Sadhus* (holy men) are a common sight in India. These two Sadhus belong to two different sects of Hinduism, as indicated by the marks on their foreheads. Generally speaking, horizontal lines indicate Vaishnava affiliation and vertical lines indicate Shaiva affiliation.

could keep in touch with the world in general, but the ascetic stayed completely away from it. Living his life with only the most basic personal items, he had no physical comfort. His whole day was devoted to meditation, reflection and the reading of Upanishadic scriptures. It was believed that this simple yet serene state of the sanyasin continues beyond death and that such people never returned to this world. Such ascetics are esteemed in Hindu society and are entitled to special respect and support.

Ashramas and varnas form two pillars of Hindu social and family systems of the sanatana dharma. Besides teaching the significance of the caste system and four stages of life, the sacred texts of the Brahmanic tradition also describe some rituals that should be performed at strategic points in a Hindu's life.

Rites of Passage

Rituals performed and celebrated at the time of important transitions in the life of a Hindu, from the moment of conception to the time of death, are called *samskara*. There are four major rites of passage, passed down in the mainstream Brahmanic tradition and described in the *Shastras*. These are the prenatal, childhood, marriage, and death rituals.

On such occasions, family members and friends join together to bless the individual and to protect him from any harm. All major rituals are performed at home. Family priests are usually called in to perform the most important rituals, but family members are usually the primary performers of the home rituals.

Prenatal Rituals

Three rites are performed before the birth of a child: the rite of conception, the wish for a male child, and protection of the fetus. To ensure the fertility and safety of the mother and child, the rite of conception is performed long before there is any news of the arrival of a child. In the third or fourth month of pregnancy, a rite is performed for procuring a male child. This ceremony also contains rites and safeguards against miscarriages. Finally, between the fourth and the eighth month of pregnancy, a rite is performed to protect the fetus from evil spirits.

Childhood Rituals

A number of rituals are performed between a child's birth and adolescence. The first is a simple ritual, performed immediately after birth. The most important is the second ritual, known as the naming ceremony, which is held on the tenth or twelfth day after the birth of the baby. On this occasion, the baby is given a formal name. The third ritual is celebrated when a baby is weaned from it's mother and given solid food to eat for the first time. This is celebrated sometime in the sixth month. Between the ages of one and five, girls experience a ceremonial ear-piercing, and the boys have their first haircut. These two ceremonies conclude the childhood rites.

Many of the childhood and adolescence rituals are aimed at protecting and nurturing the child. However, others have social significance. Through them, the young child is prepared to assume the social and religious responsibilities of the adult world.

The main ritual of adolescence is the Vedic initiation rite called *upanayana* (popularly known as the "thread ceremony"). It is regarded as the second birth of the initiate. Only male children of the upper three castes (Brahmins, Shatriyas, and Vaishyas) go through this ceremony of initiation into their respective classes.

■ *Three brothers prepare for the elaborate rite of passage called* **Upanayana,** *the "thread ceremony." Priests and family members are present at the ceremony, which is performed in front of a fire pit.*

Males who take part in the upanayana ritual are called "twice born" because they are spiritually reborn at this ceremony. Their first birth, from their mother's womb, is considered incomplete. At the upanayana ceremony, the children are "born again" as members of the Hindu social system. Members of the fourth caste, Shudras, do not go through this ceremony. Therefore they are born only physically, not spiritually, and for this reason they are not considered pure. Thus, they are not fit to do any work that is considered sacred. Before the ritual of initiation, the children of higher classes are considered the same as Shudras. Men of the three higher castes who remain uninitiated after the ages of sixteen, twenty-two, and twenty-four, respectively, are regarded as impure, and social interaction with them is forbidden.

Before the ritual of upanayana, the boy eats his last meal with his mother. From that moment, he is expected to eat with the adult male members of his family. His head is then shaved and he is bathed. He wears a girdle of deerskin (nowadays replaced by cotton material), carries a wooden staff, and is given finally the

Sacred Thread. This thread, or *upavita*, consists of three cords, each of which is made by twisting three strands. The upavita is a visible symbol of all individual existences, inseparable and linked to one single source of the universe. The thread is normally worn over the left shoulder and hangs under the right arm. It is regarded as the central element of the initiation rituals.

After the completion of this ceremony, the young man, along with the priest, puts wood into the sacred fire. This is the boy's first encounter with the sacrifice, the central religious act of the Vedic religion. Formerly, the pupil remained for many years after the ceremony at the teacher's house, away from his own home and family. During this time he had no status, rank, or property. Rather, he led a life of humility, obedience and chastity. In present times, many young men perform this ritual before they go to college, or even later, before they get married. Modern young men do not live with the teacher unless they have decided to devote their lives to the study of scriptures.

At the completion of his studies, another ritual incorporates the student into society. In modern times, this ritual takes place when a child graduates and returns to his parents' home. The central theme of this ritual is a ceremonial bath. After the bath, the student becomes a full-fledged member of the community. He is ready to marry and become a householder. The search for a suitable bride begins.

Marriage

Marriage (*vivah*) is one of the most important rituals in the life of a Hindu. Only a married man is allowed to perform principal religious sacrifices. In addition, he is the only one who takes care of family members belonging to all four ashramas of life (unmarried men are responsible only for relatives who belong to the first two ashramas). Thus, a married man's role is pivotal in Hindu society. However, such a man is considered complete only after begetting a son.

The first step in the vivah is finding a suitable match. The parents make their choice with the child's consent. Then, with the help of an astrological calendar and the family priest, they decide on a favorable day for the marriage ritual.

The betrothal takes place some time before the day of the marriage. On the wedding day, the groom goes to the bride's house in a colorful procession along with many friends and relatives. The bride wears bright red attire, symbolizing love and faith, and the groom wears white traditional dress, symbolizing purity and serenity. The father of the groom asks for the bride's hand, and the bride's father formally offers it. The marriage ritual is conducted by a family priest belonging to the Brahmin class. Although the main ritual varies from region to region, the four basic rites remain the same and form the core of the ceremony.

The rites are performed in front of a fire pit made of bricks. The priest sits close to the fire, Agni, with the bride, the groom and the parents of the bride and groom. The invited family and friends encircle this group while the priest performs the wedding rites. In the wedding ritual, as in puja, bells are rung, the Vedic hymns are chanted, and fragrant flowers, clarified butter, uncooked grain, and many other such ingredients are poured as oblations into Agni.

Amid the festive sounds, sweet smells, and vibrant colors, the bridegroom says to the bride that he will take care of her health and happiness. He then guides her three times around the fire. After each complete turn, he recites a mantra. He tells her, "Be my friend. May you be devoted to me. Let us have many sons. May they reach old age." Then the couple takes seven steps around the fire. The taking of the seven steps is the most important part of the ceremony. To symbolize their union, the bride and the groom eat a common meal while sitting together. After the marriage ritual, the couple goes to the husband's home, and on the fourth day, several rites are performed to ensure fertility.

Cremation and the Last Rites

When someone dies, family and friends are quickly informed. Within a few hours, the dead body is carried on a litter in a procession to the local cremation ground. The procession is led by the eldest son, acting as the chief mourner of the deceased. The name of a god—either Rama, Hari (Krishna), or Shiva—is cried out as the procession moves. At the cremation ground, the body is laid on a specially prepared pyre of wood and is cremated in the belief that its soul will be united with the ancestors after the proper funerary rituals are performed. The mourners return to their homes without looking back.

Cremation has been the customary way of taking care of human remains since the earliest period of Indian history. Cremation was regarded as the last sacrifice, *antyesti,* in which one's own body is offered in the sacred fire, Agni. It is believed that from the fire the deceased person is born again into a new existence in the company of his or her ancestors.

The funerary ritual, *sraddha,* is performed in order to help the deceased reach the homes of the ancestors safely. It is believed that after the cremation, the people who have died pass through a period when they live as ghosts. During this period, which may last as long as one year, they are dangerous, and their relatives are impure. Offerings of food and water are made for the newly deceased in the ritual of sraddha. Balls of rice and libations of water are offered, accompanied by the recitation of texts expressing respect and concern. The death rituals are the rites of passage from the earthly existence to the world of the fathers. They last anywhere from twelve days to a year, depending on the beliefs of the person who is performing them.

One notices a remarkable feature in all the rites of passage of Hindus—they do not refer at all to the common Hindu belief of karma, samsara, and moksha. These rites are founded on a world view that celebrates life and fertility, and when death inevitably arrives, Hindus ritually transport the dead to the world of the fathers. A significant element that is consistent from the Vedic sacrifices to the contemporary Hindu rituals is the role of fire as a central element of almost all the rites of passage.

The prenatal, childhood, marriage, and death rituals are also performed for women belonging to the twice-born castes. During these times, Vedic formulas are not recited, since women are not allowed to read or hear the *Vedas*. Indeed, within the system of varnasramadharma, women were not believed to be spiritually inclined. They did not enter into any of the stages of life, they were dependent on their fathers as young girls, on their husbands as women, and in their old age, they were the responsibility of their sons.

Months of the Hindu Lunar Calendar	
Chaitra	March/April
Vaishakha	April/May
Jyaishtha	May/June
Ashadha	June/July
Shravana	July/August
Bhadra	August/September
Ashvina	September/October
Kartika	October/November
Agrahyana	November/December
Pausa	November/December
Magha	January/February
Phalguna	February/March

Shukla Paksha is the fortnight of the waxing moon. **Krishna Paksha** is the fortnight of the waning moon.

CHAPTER 8

Innovations and Modern Hinduism

The religious life of Hindus today is devoted to Bhakti, puja, rituals and festivals performed at home and in the temple, and the varnasramadharma system. Some Hindus follow all of these traditions and others just a few. Thousands of modern Hindus practice another ancient tradition—that of devotion to saints. The saints have led the innovative movements in Hinduism.

The Role of the Saints

In Hinduism, saints have been pivotal in generating and spreading new ideas rooted in ancient traditions. The extraordinary saint-poets of the epics and the *Puranas* and the Bhakti movement made Brahmanism available to the common people. During Islamic rule, the wandering minstrels kept Hindu beliefs and traditions alive without changing its internal structure. During the nineteenth century, modern Hindus rediscovered their forgotten scriptures as they came face to face with the Industrial Revolution and Christianity. This environment led to new religious movements.

Maharishi Mahesh Yogi, a modern saint in New York, accepts flowers from his followers. Mahesh Yogi has established many meditation centers in the United States.

Each century has given rise to hundreds of such saints. Some become popular only after death, others while still alive. Some of these are much esteemed, others go unnoticed. Some are wandering mystics leading a life of asceticism, others are quite practical. Some are illiterate, others have doctorates from universities. However, all of these saints have certain things in common: they are completely devoted to the divine, have love and compassion for humanity, and are sensitive toward the universe. They see the universe as an undivided whole and human beings not as separate individuals but connected to each other through their natural and social environment. Moreover, Hindu saints see all human beings as ultimately connected with divine reality.

In the present century, many living saints look after their followers' physical and mental well-being in rapidly changing times. Their popularity is not due to their strict adherence to the ancient scriptures. Rather, it comes from their roles in bringing about relevant changes needed and desired by the common people.

One such twentieth century saint was Sri Ramana, who at the age of seventeen became troubled by the awareness of his own mortality. He lost interest in his studies and began meditating, spending most of his time at a Shiva temple. One day, while he was meditating, he went into a trance in which he received assurance that he was united with the Universal One. Sri Ramana spent the rest of his life in the Shiva temple and had many disciples whom he advised to inspect a path of self-inquiry. Sri Ramana came to be called Maharishi, meaning "great ascetic."

Modern Hindu gurus, or teacher-saints, follow one of the many religious ways, of which the path of yoga is the most common. Through the exercises of mind and body, yoga teaches techniques for achieving self-insight and mental balance. These living saints teach their followers how to gain peace, shed superficial values, become loving and compassionate, and feel one with each other and with the universe.

Conversion

The spiritual power of Hinduism and its teacher-saints has drawn many people toward this religion. In the twentieth century, people from around the world have pursued Hindu wisdom and even sought to convert to this faith. Conversions have happened, despite the fact that traditionally, a non-Hindu cannot convert to Hinduism. Hindus believe that one can only be a Hindu if one is born into a Hindu household.

It has only been possible to convert to Hinduism since the end of the nineteenth century. It was Christianity, with its missionary spirit and its idea of conversion, that influenced many Hindu reform movements. From these influences, Hindu conversions developed.

One way a non-Hindu could convert to Hinduism is by following the Hindu dharma and samsara very diligently. The convert could celebrate various Hindu ceremonies and rituals, become the student of a guru, change his or her name, and thus *work* at becoming a Hindu. Eventually, within a generation or two, through marriage and other social interactions, one could call oneself a Hindu.

This option for conversion is similar to the way in which a lower-caste family can now rise to a higher-caste. Traditionally, a non-Hindu or lower-caste family could not even interact with a Hindu family of a higher status. Recently, though, it has become possible for a low-caste family to ascend gradually to a higher caste. To do so, the family adopts the rituals, religious ceremonies, and general way of living of a higher-caste family. In addition, such an ascent is made more achievable by taking up vegetarianism, marrying into a higher caste, or both.

American Movements in Hinduism

With the new possibilities for conversion and change in caste, new trends in Hindu spirituality have developed. One noteworthy trend in this area is the zeal with which many sacred centers and research societies have grown in the United States during the last quarter century. Today there are hundreds of Hindu teacher-saints in America. The saints are both Indians who have immigrated to the United States and Americans who have trained in India.

Scholars suggest many reasons for this trend. For one thing, an extremely fast-paced lifestyle, in which bodily comforts and pleasures are never satisfied, can create physical tension and mental pressure. Such is the lifestyle of the United States. In that environment, many people seek an escape from a material world in which there seems no hope of knowing God. In addition, some scholars emphasize the American inclination for exploration and experimentation. In the past, Americans explored a new continent; now attention has shifted to the exploration of the inner self.

A "great ascetic" who brought Hinduism to the United States is Maharishi Mahesh Yogi. Mahesh Yogi is a living saint who has established many meditation centers in Europe and America. He encourages his pupils to use yoga to attain mental and physical health. His organization, the Students' International Meditation Society, is based on the ideal of emotional balance and physical well-being. In this institute, thousands of students practice meditation under the guidance of gurus. This institute has encouraged the development of study and research of yoga.

Another saint, Bhaktivedanta, has also brought Hindu teachings to the United States. Bhaktivedanta was deeply interested in scriptures from his early youth and led the life of a devoted Hindu. He was married, but at the age of fifty-four he retired from the world and adopted the life of a forest dweller in order to devote more time to study and writing. He became a *sanyasin* (ascetic) at the age of sixty-three and wrote several books. Bhaktivedanta followed the path of devotion to God by meditation and chanting.

In 1965, Bhaktivedanta came to the United States to teach Hinduism to Americans. He started a devotional movement called the International Society for Krishna Consciousness. Within a decade, he had gathered hundreds of followers who gave up their former way of life in order to be with their teacher. A magnificent memorial dedicated to him has been constructed by his disciples in Moundsville, West Virginia.

The followers of Hindu saints need not be with their gurus forever. Once they have been taught by a guru, the students are expected to go on their own. As a famous contemporary philosopher-teacher, Krishnamurti, said, "One should neither have followers nor should one follow someone. The moment you follow someone, you cease to follow Truth. . . . Truth is in everyone. No man from outside yourself can make you free."

■ *Swami Bhaktivedanta chants sacred syllables while devotees dance. The Swami came to the United States to teach Hinduism in 1965.*

In addition to following saints, many individuals interested in Hinduism work in independent research and study centers established in the United States. Ancient texts are translated, studied, and analyzed at these centers. At some centers, regular prayers or group singing sessions are held. The membership of most of these centers is made up of Americans with diverse religious backgrounds.

Hinduism, a fluid and vital religion, has adapted itself well within the novel geographical and socioeconomic environment of the United States. It has progressed very comfortably and has acquired new growth. Hindu temple complexes are located in Pittsburgh, Chicago, New York, Los Angeles, and other U.S. cities. Because of their unusual architecture, these temples have also become tourist attractions. The building of a Hindu temple by

Hindus in America represents their attempt to establish a sacred center. By building a temple, Hindus believe that a sacred space is created, and it is considered a world in itself. The temple becomes a safe space for a minority community to live and act out its identity.

One outstanding example of sacred space is the temple in Pittsburgh, Pennsylvania. This temple is based on traditional Indian architectural plans. It was established and installed by performing the rituals as prescribed in the Shilpa Shastras.

The life of the Hindu temple at Penn Hills is a characteristic example of Hinduism. Many additions, alterations, and modifications have been made to the traditional architectural plan in order for it to suit modern devotees living in a technological society. Many of the ritual practices of the temple have been adapted as well.

Although puja is held each day, major rituals are held on the weekends for the convenience of busy patrons. Certain regulations and rules observed in traditional Hindu temples have been omitted here. For one thing, the temple has a parking lot just outside its premises because the modern devotee has neither time nor energy to climb hills to visit the temple.

Although in many Hindu temples non-Hindus are not allowed near the innermost sanctuary, at Penn Hills, regular weekend tours are organized for non-Hindus. These tours aim to make visitors understand the rich meaning of the Hindu temple, its icons, and its religious rituals. A kitchen, a restaurant, and rest rooms have also been incorporated into the temple complex. Despite these apparent departures, Hindu temples in the United States are vibrant and vital places that fulfill the religious, social, and cultural need of the Hindus living in a modern, secular or non-Hindu society.

The history of Hinduism shows over and over the diverse and original ideas and beliefs of this religion. Though Hinduism is rooted in ancient values and beliefs, it is constantly incorporating new ideas. This change is evident in spiritual yogic movements brought to the West by the living saints, in the architectural innovations in the traditional temple plan, in the possibility of conversion to Hinduism by non-Hindus, and even the ascension of the hierarchical ladder or caste system.

Hinduism is the most ancient and yet the most modern of religions. It keeps itself rooted in its traditions, but its adherents force innovations through reform movements when the time requires it. Not only are many Hindu traditions such as the low status of women and low castes changing in the country of its origin, but this ancient religion is also making modifications for its expatriated devotees.

GLOSSARY

Agni—"Fire." The term also refers to the Vedic god of fire, Agni, who is the archetypal priest.

Ashrama—A forest retreat where sages, ascetics, religious teachers, and their students live. Also the term for the four stages of life.

Asura—A group of gods in constant struggle with devas. While devas were included among the Vedic gods, asuras were outsiders.

Atman—The soul of an individual. The term refers to the essence within people which is identical to the essence of the Universal Power considered as the source of everything.

Avatara—An incarnation of god who descends to earth in human or animal form to save humankind from calamities.

Bhagavad Gita—The sixth book of the epic Mahabharata in which the god Krishna teaches Arjuna about self-duty and devotion.

Bhakti—Devotion, faith, and love. Most often expressed by a complete devotion to a personal god.

Brahma—The creator god, also known as Prajapati. One of the gods of triad formed by Vishnu, Siva, and Brahma. His consort is Sarasvati the goddess of knowledge.

Brahman—The One God of Hinduism, also known as the One, the Ultimate Reality, and the World Soul. He is the self-existing Universal Power which is believed to be the source of everything.

Brahmanas—Ritual texts attached to the four Vedas.

Brahmin—The uppermost class of the Hindu caste system, whose duties are to perform rituals and to teach.

Brahmachari—The Student. This is the first of the four stages of life.

Darshana—Sacred 'Seeing' of a deity by a devotee.

Devas—A class of Vedic gods.

Dharma—Social duty or religious law. The principle of order in Hindu society and ultimately in the universe.

Gayatri—A verse devoted to the Vedic solar god Savitr. This verse is the most commonly recited by Hindus.

Grihasthin—The Householder. This is the second of the four stages of Hindu life.

Guru—A spiritual teacher who is considered to be a divine manifestation.

Jivan Mukti—A person who has attained spiritual liberation while still alive; one who is in a state of perfection and has realized unity with Brahman.

Karma—Good and bad deeds or acts in a person's previous or present life which will determine the quality of the next incarnation.

Linga—Phallus. The male generative organ that symbolizes Shiva's erotic power as well as his ascetic power.

Mandira—The Hindu temple.

Mantra—A sacred formula, syllable, or utterance, usually a ritual statement or verse-prayer.

Maya—The illusion one has that this transitory world is permanent while living in it.

Moksha—Enlightenment. Release.

Mudra—Symbolic hand gestures, the origin of which lies in Indian classical dance. They are also extensively used in creating sacred images.

Murti—The artistic representations of Hindu deities which, after ritual consecration, become the focus of worship.

Polytheism—The belief in many gods.

Prasada—The food offered to deities by devotees which is blessed by the deities, returned to the devotees, and eventually consumed by the devotees.

Puja—Worship in which a deity is honored by the offerings of flowers, incense, food, etc.

Pujari—Brahmin priest who performs the Puja.

Rishi—Sages who had perceived the Ultimate Reality and who revealed the texts of the Upanishads.

Rita—The Vedic term for the cosmic and ethical order of things, the later extension of which is the concept of Dharma.

Samsara—The cycles of a soul's birth and rebirth through different lifetimes. Reincarnation.

Samskara—Rites of passage.

Shaiva—The name of the cult of Shiva and his followers.

Shakta—The name for the cult of Mahadevi Shakti and her followers.

Shakti—The Great Goddess as energy and power.

Shatriya—The second highest caste, the warriors, whose duty is to fight and defend.

Vahana—"Vehicle." The term used to describe a god's means of transportation.

Veda—Earliest Hindu texts, composed before, during, and after the Aryan invasion of the Indus Valley.

FOR FURTHER READING

Barrett, Douglas, and Gray, Basil. *Indian Painting.* Macmillan London Ltd., 1978.

Basham, A.L. *The Wonder That Was India.* Fontana Books in association with Rupa & Co., 1974.

Craven, Roy C. *Indian Art.* New York: Thames and Hudson, 1987.

De Bary, Wm. Theodore, *Sources of Indian Tradition, Vols I & II.* New York: Columbia University Press, 1958.

Eck, Diana L. *Darsana: Seeing the Divine Image in India.* Anima Books, 1985.

Fenton, John Y. *Religions of Asia.* New York: St. Martin Press, 1974.

Hopkins, Thomas J. *The Hindu Religious Traditions.* California: Dickenson Publishing Company, Inc., 1971.

Huntington, Susan L. *The Art of Ancient India.* New York: Weatherhill, 1985.

Ions, Veronica. *Indian Mythology.* Paul Hamlyn Publishing Group Ltd., 1968.

Kramrisch, Stella. *Manifestations of Shiva.* Philadelphia Museum of Art, 1981.

Michell, George. *The Hindu Temple: An Introduction to its Meaning and Form.* Chicago: The University of Chicago Press, 1988.

Noss D.S., and Noss J.B. *Man's Religions.* New York: Macmillan Publishing Company, 1980.

Ramanujan, A.K. *Speaking of Siva.* New York: Penguin Books Inc., 1973.

INDEX